Outlook 2007: Basic

Student Manual

COURSE TECHNOLOGY

Australia • Canada • Mexico • Singapore
Spain • United Kingdom • United States

Outlook 2007: Basic

VP and GM, Training Group:	Michael Springer
Series Product Managers:	Charles G. Blum and Adam A. Wilcox
Writer:	Linda Long
Developmental Editor:	Kevin Ogburn
Copyeditor:	Cathy Albano
Keytester:	Cliff Coryea
Series Designer:	Adam A. Wilcox
Cover Designer:	Abby Scholz

For more information contact:

Course Technology
25 Thomson Place
Boston, MA 02210

Or find us on the Web at: www.course.com

For permission to use material from this text or product, submit a request online at: www.thomsonrights.com

Any additional questions about permissions can be submitted by e-mail to: thomsonrights@thomson.com

Trademarks

Course ILT is a trademark of Course Technology.

Microsoft is a trademark or registered trademark of Microsoft Corporation in the United States and/or other countries.

Some of the product names and company names used in this book have been used for identification purposes only and may be trademarks or registered trademarks of their respective manufacturers and sellers.

Disclaimers

Course Technology reserves the right to revise this publication and make changes from time to time in its content without notice.

Course Technology is independent from Microsoft Corporation, and not affiliated with Microsoft in any manner. While this publication may be used in assisting individuals to prepare for a Microsoft Business Certification exam, Microsoft, its dedicated program administrator, and Course Technology do not warrant that use of this publication will ensure passing a Microsoft Business Certification exam.

Student Manual
ISBN-10: 1-4239-1819-3
ISBN-13: 978-1-4239-1819-6

Student Manual with data CD and CBT
ISBN-10: 1-4239-1821-5
ISBN-13: 978-1-4239-1821-9

Printed in the United States of America

1 2 3 4 5 GLOB 09 08 07

What is the Microsoft Business Certification Program?

The Microsoft Business Certification Program enables candidates to show that they have something exceptional to offer—proven expertise in Microsoft Office programs. The two certification tracks allow candidates to choose how they want to exhibit their skills, either through validating skills within a specific Microsoft product or taking their knowledge to the next level and combining Microsoft programs to show that they can apply multiple skill sets to complete more complex office tasks. Recognized by businesses and schools around the world, over 3 million certifications have been obtained in over 100 different countries. The Microsoft Business Certification Program is the only Microsoft-approved certification program of its kind.

What is the Microsoft Certified Application Specialist Certification?

The Microsoft Certified Application Specialist Certification exams focus on validating specific skill sets within each of the Microsoft® Office system programs. The candidate can choose which exam(s) they want to take according to which skills they want to validate. The available Application Specialist exams include:

- Using Microsoft® Windows Vista™
- Using Microsoft® Office Word 2007
- Using Microsoft® Office Excel® 2007
- Using Microsoft® Office PowerPoint® 2007
- Using Microsoft® Office Access 2007
- Using Microsoft® Office Outlook® 2007

What is the Microsoft Certified Application Professional Certification?

The Microsoft Certified Application Professional Certification exams focus on a candidate's ability to use the 2007 Microsoft® Office system to accomplish industry-agnostic functions, for example Budget Analysis and Forecasting, or Content Management and Collaboration. The available Application Professional exams currently include:

- Organizational Support
- Creating and Managing Presentations
- Content Management and Collaboration
- Budget Analysis and Forecasting

What do the Microsoft Business Certification Vendor of Approved Courseware logos represent?

Microsoft
CERTIFIED
Application Specialist

Approved Courseware

Microsoft
CERTIFIED
Application Professional

Approved Courseware

The logos validate that the courseware has been approved by the Microsoft® Business Certification Vendor program and that these courses cover objectives that will be included in the relevant exam. It also means that after utilizing this courseware, you may be prepared to pass the exams required to become a Microsoft Certified Application Specialist or Microsoft Certified Application Professional.

For more information

To learn more about the Microsoft Certified Application Specialist or Professional exams[1], visit www.microsoft.com/learning/msbc.

To learn about other Microsoft Certified Application Specialist approved courseware from Course Technology, visit www.courseilt.com.

[1]The availability of Microsoft Certified Application exams varies by Microsoft Office program, program version, and language. Visit www.microsoft.com/learning for exam availability.

Contents

Introduction

After reading this introduction, you'll know how to:

A Use Course Technology ILT manuals in general.

B Use prerequisites, a target student description, course objectives, and a skills inventory to set your expectations properly for the course.

C Re-key this course after class.

Topic A: About the manual

Course Technology ILT philosophy

Course Technology ILT manuals facilitate your learning by providing structured interaction with the software itself. While we provide text to explain difficult concepts, the hands-on activities are the focus of our courses. By paying close attention as your instructor leads you through these activities, you'll learn the skills and concepts effectively.

We believe strongly in the instructor-led classroom. During class, focus on your instructor. Our manuals are designed and written to facilitate your interaction with your instructor, and not to call attention to manuals themselves.

We believe in the basic approach of setting expectations, delivering instruction, and providing summary and review afterwards. For this reason, lessons begin with objectives and end with summaries. We also provide overall course objectives and a course summary to provide both an introduction to and closure on the entire course.

Manual components

The manuals contain these major components:

- Table of contents
- Introduction
- Units
- Course summary
- Quick reference
- Glossary
- Index

Each element is described below.

Table of contents

The table of contents acts as a learning roadmap.

Introduction

The introduction contains information about our training philosophy and our manual components, features, and conventions. It contains target student, prerequisite, objective, and setup information for the specific course.

Units

Units are the largest structural component of the course content. A unit begins with a title page that lists objectives for each major subdivision, or topic, within the unit. Within each topic, conceptual and explanatory information alternates with hands-on activities. Units conclude with a summary comprising one paragraph for each topic, and an independent practice activity that gives you an opportunity to practice the skills you've learned.

The conceptual information takes the form of text paragraphs, exhibits, lists, and tables. The activities are structured in two columns, one telling you what to do, the other providing explanations, descriptions, and graphics.

Course summary

This section provides a text summary of the entire course. It's useful for providing closure at the end of the course. The course summary also indicates the next course in this series, if there is one, and lists additional resources you might find useful as you continue to learn about the software.

Quick reference

The quick reference is an at-a-glance job aid summarizing some of the more common features of the software.

Glossary

The glossary provides definitions for all of the key terms used in this course.

Index

The index at the end of this manual makes it easy for you to find information about a particular software component, feature, or concept.

Manual conventions

We've tried to keep the number of elements and the types of formatting to a minimum in the manuals. This aids in clarity and makes the manuals more classically elegant looking. But there are some conventions and icons you should know about.

Convention	Description
Italic text	In conceptual text, indicates a new term or feature.
Bold text	In unit summaries, indicates a key term or concept. In an independent practice activity, indicates an explicit item that you select, choose, or type.
`Code font`	Indicates code or syntax.
`Longer strings of ▶ code will look ▶ like this.`	In the hands-on activities, any code that's too long to fit on a single line is divided into segments by one or more continuation characters (▶). This code should be entered as a continuous string of text.
Select **bold item**	In the left column of hands-on activities, bold sans-serif text indicates an explicit item that you select, choose, or type.
Keycaps like (↵ ENTER)	Indicate a key on the keyboard you must press.

Hands-on activities

The hands-on activities are the most important parts of our manuals. They're divided into two primary columns. The "Here's how" column gives short instructions to you about what to do. The "Here's why" column provides explanations, graphics, and clarifications. Here's a sample:

Do it!

A-1:   Creating a commission formula

Here's how	Here's why
1 Open Sales	This is an oversimplified sales compensation worksheet. It shows sales totals, commissions, and incentives for five sales reps.
2 Observe the contents of cell F4	F4 ▼ = =E4*C_Rate
	The commission rate formulas use the name "C_Rate" instead of a value for the commission rate.

For these activities, we have provided a collection of data files designed to help you learn each skill in a real-world business context. As you work through the activities, you will modify and update these files. Of course, you might make a mistake and, therefore, want to re-key the activity starting from scratch. To make it easy to start over, you will rename each data file at the end of the first activity in which the file is modified. Our convention for renaming files is to add the word "My" to the beginning of the file name. In the above activity, for example, a file called "Sales" is being used for the first time. At the end of this activity, you would save the file as "My sales," thus leaving the "Sales" file unchanged. If you make a mistake, you can start over using the original "Sales" file.

In some activities, however, it may not be practical to rename the data file. If you want to retry one of these activities, ask your instructor for a fresh copy of the original data file.

Topic B: Setting your expectations

Properly setting your expectations is essential to your success. This topic will help you do that by providing:

- Prerequisites for this course
- A description of the target student at whom the course is aimed
- A list of the objectives for the course
- A skills assessment for the course

Course prerequisites

Before taking this course, you should be familiar with personal computers and the use of a keyboard and a mouse. Furthermore, this course assumes that you've completed the *Windows XP: Basic* course (or *Windows Vista: Basic*) or have equivalent experience.

Target student

The target student for the course is an individual who wants to learn the basic features of Outlook 2007 to create and use messages, appointments, tasks, and other Outlook items.

Microsoft Certified Application Specialist certification

This course is designed to help you pass the Microsoft Certified Application Specialist exam for Outlook 2007. For comprehensive certification training, you should complete all of the following courses:

- *Outlook 2007: Basic*
- *Outlook 2007: Intermediate*
- *Outlook 2007: Advanced*

Course objectives

These overall course objectives will give you an idea about what to expect from the course. It's also possible that they'll help you see that this course isn't the right one for you. If you think you either lack the prerequisite knowledge or already know most of the subject matter to be covered, you should let your instructor know that you think you are misplaced in the class.

Note: In addition to the general objectives listed below, specific Microsoft Certified Application Specialist exam objectives are listed at the beginning of each topic (where applicable). To download a complete mapping of exam objectives to ILT Series content, go to: www.virtualrom.com/64EC67739

After completing this course, you'll know how to:

- Explore the Outlook environment; use Outlook's features; use and customize Outlook Today; and use the different help options.

- Configure different e-mail accounts; use the Inbox to read, create, and send messages; reply to, format, and check spelling of messages; preview, read, and save attachments; and forward, delete, and move messages.

- Set delivery options for messages, flag messages, set up the read receipt option for messages, specify e-mail security settings, specify options for controlling junk e-mail, set up Search Folders, and print messages.

- Use the Contacts folder to manage e-mail addresses and create distribution lists; and create, edit, format, and send electronic business cards.

- Use the Tasks folder to add, edit, and mark tasks; assign tasks; accept or decline a task request; send an update; and track an assigned task.

- Create and organize your appointments by using the Calendar; explore Calendar views; modify, edit, and delete appointments; and add multi-day and annual events to the Calendar.

- Use the Calendar to schedule a meeting, and use the meeting workspace; read and respond to meeting requests; and review, modify, and cancel a meeting.

Skills inventory

Use the following form to gauge your skill level entering the class. For each skill listed, rate your familiarity from 1 to 5, with 5 being the most familiar. *This is not a test.* Rather, it is intended to provide you with an idea of where you're starting from at the beginning of class. If you're wholly unfamiliar with all the skills, you might not be ready for the class. If you think you already understand all of the skills, you might need to move on to the next course in the series. In either case, you should let your instructor know as soon as possible.

Skill	1	2	3	4	5
Exploring the Outlook window and the Navigation pane					
Using the Reading pane					
Using the To-Do bar					
Accessing folders from Outlook Today					
Customizing Outlook Today					
Using the Type a question for help box					
Using the Outlook Help window					
Configuring an Outlook Anywhere connection					
Configuring a Hotmail account					
Configuring a POP3 account					
Previewing and reading a message					
Creating, formatting, and sending a message					
Checking a message's spelling					
Replying to and forwarding a message					
Resending a message					
Saving a message as a file					
Deleting and restoring a message					
Sending and forwarding attachments					
Compressing large image attachments					
Previewing and saving an attachment					
Defining delivery options					
Flagging an e-mail message					

Skill	1	2	3	4	5
Using delivery and read receipts					
Restricting messages					
Digitally signing a message					
Sending an encrypted message					
Adding senders to the Blocked Senders list or to the Safe Senders list					
Marking a message as not junk					
Changing junk e-mail options					
Setting up and using a search folder					
Customizing page setup for printing					
Printing a message					
Adding a new contact					
Modifying a contact					
Attaching items to a contact					
Adding a contact from the same company					
Sending and saving contacts					
Creating and using a distribution list					
Updating a distribution list					
Creating an electronic business card					
Modifying and formatting an electronic business card					
Sending an electronic business card					
Creating a contact from an electronic business card					
Creating and deleting tasks					
Editing a task					
Adding a recurring task					
Marking a task as completed					
Attaching a task to a message					
Assigning a task					

Skill	1	2	3	4	5
Accepting a task request					
Sending a task status report					
Tracking an assigned task					
Setting up an appointment					
Adding a recurring appointment					
Inserting an appointment into a message					
Modifying a recurring appointment					
Deleting and restoring an appointment					
Changing the work day times					
Displaying multiple time zones					
Changing your time zone					
Adding events					
Adding holidays to the calendar					
Planning a meeting					
Creating and sending a meeting request					
Adding a recurring meeting					
Modifying a recurring meeting					
Reading and accepting a meeting request					
Receiving a New Time Proposed message					
Declining a meeting request					
Reviewing meeting responses					
Updating a meeting					
Adding meeting attendees					
Canceling a meeting					

Topic C: Re-keying the course

If you have the proper hardware and software, you can re-key this course after class. This section explains what you need in order to do so and how to do it.

Hardware requirements

Your personal computer should have:

- A keyboard and a mouse
- A Pentium 500 MHz processor (or higher)
- 256 MB RAM (or higher)
- 3 GB available hard disk space
- A CD-ROM drive
- An SVGA at 1024 × 768, or higher resolution monitor
- A connection to a network printer
- A network card and relevant cabling

Software requirements

You will also need the following software:

- Windows XP with Service Pack 2 or Windows Vista
- Microsoft Office Outlook 2007, Microsoft Office Word 2007, and Microsoft Office Excel 2007

Network requirements

The following network components and connectivity are also required for this course:

- Internet access, for the following purposes:
    - Downloading the latest critical updates and service packs from www.windowsupdate.com
    - Completing activities A-2 and A-3 in the unit titled "E-mail" and activities B-2 and B-3 in the unit titled "E-mail management"
    - Downloading the student data files from www.courseilt.com (if necessary)
- Hotmail and POP3 Internet accounts are needed for each student to complete activities A-2 and A-3 in the unit titled "E-mail"

Setup instructions to re-key the course

Because this course requires an Exchange server and other Outlook clients, it would be impossible to duplicate the classroom setup on your own. If you have Outlook 2007 and Word 2007, you can re-key the activities, but keep in mind that the contents of your Inbox and other Outlook folders will differ from those shown in this manual.

Before you re-key the course, you will need to perform the following steps.

1   Create a folder called Student Data at the root directory of the hard drive.

2   Download the student data examples for the course (if you do not have an Internet connection, you can ask your instructor for a copy of the data files on a diskette).

    a   Connect to www.courseilt.com/instructor_tools.html.

    b   Click the link for Microsoft Outlook 2007 to display a page of course listings, and then click the link for Outlook 2007: Basic.

    c   Click the link for downloading the data disk files, and follow the instructions that appear on your screen.

3   Copy the data files to the Student Data folder.

CertBlaster exam preparation software

If you plan to take the Microsoft Certified Application Specialist exam for Outlook 2007, we encourage you to use the CertBlaster pre- and post-assessment software that comes with this course. To download and install your free software:

1   Go to www.courseilt.com/certblaster.

2   Click the link for Outlook 2007.

3   Save the .EXE file to a folder on your hard drive. (Note: If you skip this step, the CertBlaster software will not install correctly.)

4   Click Start and choose Run.

5   Click Browse and then navigate to the folder that contains the .EXE file.

6   Select the .EXE file and click Open.

7   Click OK and follow the on-screen instructions. When prompted for the password, enter **c_604**.

Unit 1

Getting started

Unit time: 50 minutes

Complete this unit, and you'll know how to:

A Identify the components of the Outlook environment, and use Outlook panes and folders.

B Use Outlook Today to keep track of your schedule and tasks for today, and customize the Outlook Today page.

C Get help by using the Type a question for help box and the Microsoft Office Outlook Help window.

Topic A: The program window

This topic covers the following Microsoft Certified Application Specialist exam objectives for Outlook 2007.

#	Objective
1.7.1	Show, hide, or move the reading pane
5.6.1	Show, hide, or minimize the To Do bar • Minimize the To Do bar

Outlook overview

Explanation   Outlook is a Microsoft mail application that you can use to send and receive e-mail. *E-mail* is an electronic message sent from one computer to another. You can also use Outlook as a personal organizer to schedule meetings, appointments, and tasks.

Any e-mail message, contact, or task created in Outlook is called an *item*. Items are stored in folders, such as Inbox, Calendar, Contacts, Tasks, and Notes. These folders help you organize information. You can access the items within each folder by using the buttons available in the Outlook window.

Starting the application

You can start Outlook by clicking Start and then choosing All Programs, Microsoft Office, Microsoft Office Outlook 2007. You can also start Outlook by double-clicking the Microsoft Office Outlook icon on the desktop.

Outlook window elements

The Outlook window contains elements that are common to other Windows-based applications. These elements include a control menu icon, a title bar, a menu bar, a Standard toolbar, and a status bar, as shown in Exhibit 1-1.

Control menu icon   Menu bar   Title bar

Standard toolbar

Status bar

Exhibit 1-1: The Outlook window—common window elements

The following table describes the common Windows-based elements of the Outlook window (shown in Exhibit 1-1):

Element	Description
Control menu icon	Displays commands used to work with the main program menu.
Menu bar	Contains menus such as File, Edit, and View.
Title bar	Displays the name of the active folder (by default, Inbox) followed by the name of the program.
Standard toolbar	Contains buttons that you can use instead of menu options to perform common tasks. The buttons available on the Standard toolbar depend on the active folder.
Status bar	Displays information about the current state of what is being viewed in the window.

The Outlook window also contains elements that are specific to the Outlook application. These elements include a Navigation pane, a Folder pane, a Reading pane and a To-Do bar, as shown in Exhibit 1-2. The Navigation pane is made up of three sections: the active pane, pane-switching buttons and icons, and a Configure Buttons icon. The Folder pane displays the Folder Contents list. The Reading Pane displays e-mail messages. The To-Do bar displays the Date Navigator, upcoming appointments, and tasks.

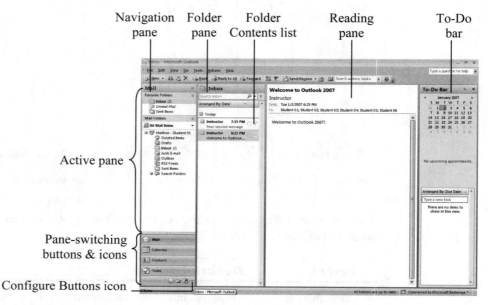

Exhibit 1-2: The Outlook window—Outlook-specific elements

The following table describes the common elements of the Outlook program window (shown in Exhibit 1-2).

Element	Description
Navigation pane	Provides centralized navigation to all parts of Outlook. Displays the active pane, pane-switching buttons and icons, and the Configure Buttons icon. Replaces the Outlook Bar used in previous versions of Outlook.
Pane-switching buttons and icons	Displays commonly used panes (such as Mail, Calendar, and Notes) with one click.
Configure Buttons icon	Displays commands used to change the appearance of the Navigation pane.
Folder pane	Displays the name of the active folder.
Folder Contents list	Displays the contents of the active folder.
Reading pane	Displays the contents of the selected e-mail message. Replaces the Preview Pane used in previous versions of Outlook.
To-Do bar	Displays the Date Navigator, upcoming appointments, and tasks.

Resizing a pane

You can increase or decrease the width of an individual pane in the program window. To adjust a pane's width, point to the border of the pane so that the pointer appears as a double-headed arrow, and then drag the border to the left or right.

Do it!

A-1:   Exploring the Outlook window

Here's how	Here's why
1 Click **Start** and choose **All Programs**, **Microsoft Office, Microsoft Office Outlook 2007**	To start Microsoft Outlook.
2 Maximize the Outlook window	Click the Maximize button at the top-right of the Outlook window.
3 Observe the window	(As shown in Exhibit 1-1 and Exhibit 1-2.) The Outlook window contains multiple elements, such as the title bar, the menu bar, the Folder pane, the Navigation pane, the Reading pane, and the To-Do bar.
4 Observe the Folder pane	It displays the name of the active folder. The Folder pane also contains a search box that you can use to find items in the folder.
5 Observe the Navigation pane	It displays the active pane, and it contains buttons such as Mail, Contacts, and Tasks that you can use to access other panes and folders in Outlook.
Point to the right border of the Navigation pane	The pointer's shape changes to a double-headed arrow.
Drag the border to the right	To increase the width of the Navigation pane.
Point as shown	(The Configure Buttons icon is in the Navigation pane's bottom-right corner.) You use the Configure Buttons icon to add or remove buttons in the Navigation pane.
6 Observe the Reading pane	It displays the contents of the active message in the Inbox. Notice that the Mail pane is the default active pane in the Navigation pane.

7 Click the chevron above the To-Do Bar, as shown	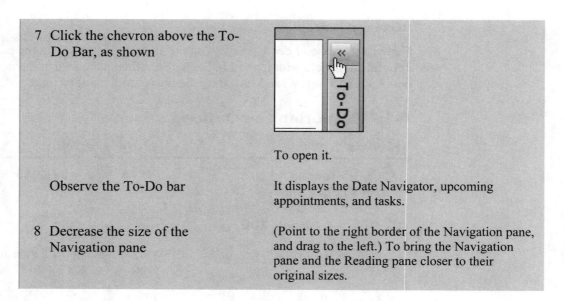
	To open it.
Observe the To-Do bar	It displays the Date Navigator, upcoming appointments, and tasks.
8 Decrease the size of the Navigation pane	(Point to the right border of the Navigation pane, and drag to the left.) To bring the Navigation pane and the Reading pane closer to their original sizes.

The Navigation pane

Explanation

The Navigation pane provides centralized navigation to all parts of Outlook. The Navigation pane has three sections, as shown in Exhibit 1-3. The top section displays the active Outlook pane, the middle section contains the pane-switching buttons, and the bottom section contains additional pane icons and the Configure Buttons icon.

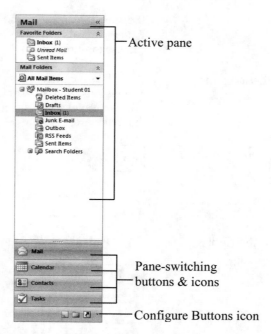

Exhibit 1-3: The Navigation pane with the Mail pane active

Default panes

Outlook provides several default panes where you can access folders or shortcuts specific to each pane. You can access each pane by clicking the pane-switching buttons and icons in the Navigation pane, as shown in Exhibit 1-3. The following panes are available by default: Mail, Calendar, Contacts, Tasks, Notes, Folder list, and Shortcuts. You can add the Journal pane using the Configure Buttons icon.

The following table describes the available panes.

Pane	Description
Mail	Displays your Favorite Folders, which includes your Inbox and Sent Items. Also displays All Mail Folders, including your Personal Folders and Search Folders.
Calendar	Displays the Date Navigator, which is a small calendar that displays the current month. Also displays links to your Calendar folders and options for changing the layout of the current view. There are links you can use to open a Shared Calendar folder.
Contacts	Displays links to your Contacts folders and options for changing the layout of the current view. There are links you can use to open a Shared Contacts folder or to customize the current view.
Tasks	Displays links to your Tasks folders and options for changing the layout of the current view. There are links you can use to open a Shared Tasks folder or to customize the current view.
Notes	Displays links to your Notes folders and options for changing the layout of the current view. There are links you can use to open a Shared Notes folder or to customize the current view.
Folder list	Displays all your folders, including Public Folders. There are links you can use to display folder size and to manage your Outlook data files.
Shortcuts	Contains links to Outlook Today and Microsoft Office Online. Shortcuts or groups that you previously added to the Outlook bar in previous versions of Outlook are automatically migrated to the Shortcuts pane when you upgrade to Office 2007.
Journal	Displays links to your Journal folders and options for changing the layout of the current view. There are links you can use to open a Shared Journal folder or to customize the current view.

Collapsing and expanding the Navigation pane

You can free up space in your Outlook window by collapsing the Navigation pane. To collapse or expand the Navigation pane, click the chevrons (arrows) at the top corner of the pane, or choose View, Navigation pane, and then choose either Normal or Collapsed. The collapsed Navigation pane, as shown in Exhibit 1-4, still provides access to the folders and files that you use most often. To view the Folder list when the Navigation pane is collapsed, click the Navigation Pane button.

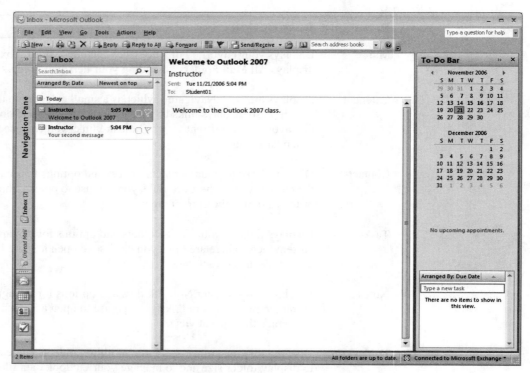

Exhibit 1-4: Collapsed Navigation pane

Viewing ScreenTips

By default, some of the pane-switching icons are located at the bottom of the Navigation pane. You can view the names of these buttons as ScreenTips by pointing to the icons, as shown in Exhibit 1-5.

Exhibit 1-5: Using ScreenTips to display the name of pane icons

Do it!   **A-2:   Examining the Navigation pane**

Here's how	Here's why
1 Click **Mail**	(If necessary.) To activate the Mail pane. Notice that the contents of the Mail pane are divided into Favorite Folders and All Mail Folders.
2 Click **Tasks**	(The Tasks button is in the Navigation pane.) To display the Task pane and the contents of the Tasks folder. Notice that there is no task present. By default, the Tasks folder is empty.
3 Click as shown	
	(Click the chevron at the top of the pane.) To collapse the Navigation pane.
Click as shown	
	To display the Task list.
Expand the Navigation pane	Click the chevron at the top of the pane.
4 Observe the icons at the bottom of the Navigation pane	There are several pane-switching icons and the Configure Buttons icon.
Point to each of the icons	To view the ScreenTips showing the names of the pane-switching icons.
5 Click	(The Notes icon is in the Navigation pane.) A blank area appears to the right in the Outlook window.
6 Click	(The Shortcuts icon is in the Navigation pane.) The shortcuts menu is empty by default, but contains buttons for adding a new group or shortcut.
7 Click	(The Folder list icon is in the Navigation pane.) To display the default Outlook folders.

Outlook folders

Explanation

Outlook provides folders in which you can save and store the items you create. You can access these folders by using the default panes in the Navigation pane. You can also access a folder by clicking the Folder list icon in the Navigation pane and then clicking the folder you want, as shown in Exhibit 1-6. You can either use the default folders in Outlook or create your own folders.

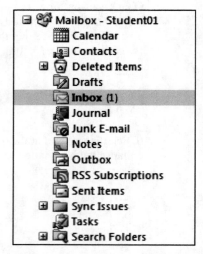

Exhibit 1-6: Default Outlook folders

The following table describes the default folders.

Folder	Description
Mailbox - <Name>	Displays the Outlook Today page, which provides a snapshot view of your activities planned for the day. If Outlook is not connected to an Exchange Server, this folder will be named Personal Folders instead of Mailbox.
Calendar	Helps you plan and schedule work-related and personal activities, such as appointments, meetings, and events.
Contacts	Stores information about people with whom you frequently communicate.
Deleted Items	Stores items that have been deleted from all the folders.
Drafts	Stores unfinished items.
Inbox	You can create, send, receive, delete, and move messages from the Inbox.
Journal	Helps you keep a record of any interaction that you want to remember. Stores actions that you choose relating to your contacts and places the actions in a timeline view.
Junk E-mail	Stores messages that were caught by the Junk E-mail filter.
Notes	Provides a facility to keep reminders about important activities to complete and meetings to attend.
Outbox	Stores items created offline that you want to send the next time you are online.

Folder	Description
RSS Subscriptions	Stores RSS (Really Simple Syndication) subscriptions so you can view data feeds from various news sources and Web logs (blogs).
Sent Items	Stores copies of items you sent to other people.
Sync Issues	Stores errors that occur when synchronizing Exchange mailbox files with local mailbox files.
Tasks	Provides a facility to create and manage the various activities you have to perform.
Search Folders	Displays the results of previously defined search queries.

Do it!

A-3: Accessing folders

Here's how	Here's why
1 Click **Mail**	To activate the Mail pane and display the Inbox folder.
Observe the Outlook window	Inbox is the active folder. The Standard toolbar contains buttons that help you compose and send e-mail. If you want to compose or send a message, you need to click the relevant button.
2 Click 🗀	The Folder list icon is in the Navigation pane.
3 In the Folder list pane, click **Calendar**	(The Calendar icon is in the Folder List pane.) To activate the Calendar pane and display the Calendar folder. The Calendar folder appears to the right of the Navigation pane. You can use the Calendar to schedule your activities, appointments, and events.
Observe the Standard toolbar	Notice that the Today button is active. The buttons on the Standard toolbar change according to the active folder. Currently, the toolbar contains buttons for tasks that can be performed by using the Calendar.
4 In the Navigation pane, click the Contacts pane-switching button	To activate the Contacts pane and display the Contacts folder. The Contacts pane displays the views for the Contacts folder. This folder is empty by default.

The Advanced toolbar

Explanation

You can view the advanced options for a specific pane or folder by using the Advanced toolbar. The Advanced toolbar contains the buttons specific to each folder. The Advanced toolbar also contains buttons, such as Back and Forward, that are common to all folders. The Advanced toolbar for the Mail pane is shown in Exhibit 1-7 as it appears when undocked. By default, the Advanced toolbar is docked at the top of the window, and the Advanced title is not displayed above the toolbar buttons.

Exhibit 1-7: The Mail pane's Advanced toolbar

To display or hide the Advanced toolbar, either choose View, Toolbars, Advanced or right-click the Standard toolbar and choose Advanced from the shortcut menu.

Using a shortcut menu

Shortcut menus provide an efficient way for you to access the operations available for an item. Shortcut menus eliminate the need for you to move your pointer to the menu bar or a toolbar. Right-click an item to view its shortcut menu. The shortcut menu displays the most common commands for that item.

Working with toolbars

You can move a toolbar by pointing to the vertical bar on the left side of the toolbar and dragging it to the left or right. You can create a floating toolbar by dragging it away from the toolbar area. To dock a floating toolbar, drag it by its title bar back to the toolbar area.

Do it!

A-4: Using the Advanced toolbar

Here's how	Here's why
1 Click 🗀	The Folder List icon is in the Navigation pane.
2 In the Folder List pane, click **Calendar**	The Calendar appears to the right in the Outlook window.
3 Choose **View**, **Toolbars**, **Advanced**	To open the Advanced toolbar. It contains buttons that help you move to the next or previous item, move a folder up by one level, and display the Outlook Today page.
4 Drag the Advanced toolbar down	(Point to its left edge and drag.) To undock it so that it becomes a floating toolbar, as shown in Exhibit 1-7. You can position a floating toolbar anywhere on the screen, but it overlaps items beneath it.
5 Drag the Advanced toolbar below the Standard toolbar	(Drag it by its title bar.) To dock it below the Standard toolbar.
6 Right-click the Standard toolbar	To display the shortcut menu. You can use any toolbar's shortcut menu to hide or show any toolbar.
Click **Advanced**	To close the Advanced toolbar.

The Reading pane

Explanation

The Reading pane is displayed only when a mail-related pane or folder is active. When the Mail pane is active, the Reading pane appears between the Folder pane and the To-Do bar in the Outlook window, as shown in Exhibit 1-8. In the Reading pane, you can read the contents of an item, preview and open attachments, follow a hyperlink, use voting buttons, and respond to meeting requests.

Show, hide, or move the Reading pane

If the Reading pane is not displayed, choose View, Reading Pane, and then select the position where you want the Reading pane displayed. To turn off the Reading pane, choose View, Reading Pane, Off.

You can also change the Reading Pane's position. The default position is to the right of the Folder pane. You can change the position to the bottom of the screen by choosing View, Reading Pane, Bottom.

Mail pane   Folder pane   Reading pane   To-Do bar

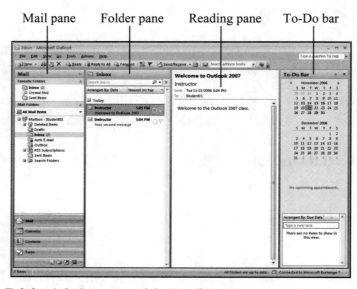

Exhibit 1-8: Location of the Reading pane

Do it!   **A-5: Using the Reading pane**

Here's how	Here's why
1 Activate Mail	Click the Mail button in the Navigation pane.
2 Click as shown	
	(The message is in the Folder Contents list.) To select the message with the subject "Welcome to Outlook 2007" from the Instructor.
Observe the Reading pane	A preview of the message content automatically appears in the Reading pane.
3 Choose **View**, **Reading Pane**, **Bottom**	The Reading pane appears at the bottom of your window.
4 Choose **View**, **Reading Pane**, **Off**	To close the Reading pane.
Choose **View**, **Reading Pane**, **Right**	To show the Reading pane in its default position.
5 In the Mail pane, click **Sent Items**	To display the contents of the Sent Items folder. The folder is empty, and the Reading pane is blank.

The To-Do bar

Explanation

The To-Do bar provides a way to view your appointments, meetings, and to-do items in a centralized list. A to-do item is any Outlook item, such as a task, an e-mail message, or a contact, that has been flagged for follow-up. By default, all tasks are flagged for follow-up when they are created. Therefore, whenever you create a task, a to-do item is automatically created.

The To-Do bar has three sections, as shown in Exhibit 1-9.

- The top section displays the Date Navigator.
- The second section displays your upcoming appointments and meetings.
- The third section displays the Task Input panel and your task list.

Exhibit 1-9: The To-Do bar

Working with the To-Do bar

The To-Do bar is turned on by default. You can turn off the To-Do bar by choosing View, To-Do Bar, Off. To turn the To-Do bar back on choose View, To-Do Bar, Normal.

If you need a larger Reading pane to read your messages, you can minimize the To-Do bar by choosing View, To-Do bar, Minimized. To expand the To-Do bar, click the chevron button at the top of the minimized bar.

Do it!   **A-6:   Using the To-Do bar**

Here's how	Here's why
1 In the Task Input panel, type **Outlook 2007 Class**	Outlook 2007 Class |
	(In the To-Do bar.) You'll create a new task for tomorrow.
Press (↵ ENTER)	The task appears in the Task list under Today.
2 Right-click the task	To display a shortcut menu. You'll change the follow-up date for the task.
Choose **Follow Up**, **Tomorrow**	The task now appears in the Task list under Tomorrow.
3 In the Date Navigator, select tomorrow's date	Notice that the task appears in the Daily Tasks list.
4 Right-click the task	To display the task shortcut menu.
Choose **Delete**	To delete the task from your Task list.
5 In the Navigation Pane, click **Mail**	The task is gone from the To-Do bar.
6 Choose **View**, **To-Do bar**, **Off**	To turn off the To-Do bar.
7 Choose **View**, **To-Do bar**, **Minimized**	To display the To-Do bar in its minimized state.
8 Click as shown	« To-Do Bar
	To return the To-Do bar to its normal state.

Topic B: Outlook Today

Explanation

Outlook Today is another way to view a summary of your activities scheduled for the day. The summary displays your events, appointments, meetings, and tasks for the day. To display the contents of the Outlook Today folder, you can either click the Outlook Today button on the Advanced toolbar, or click the Mailbox – Username folder in Mail or Folders view.

The Outlook Today page

The Outlook Today page displays the contents of the Outlook Today folder. This page appears in the Folder pane and contains three sections—Calendar, Tasks, and Messages—as shown in Exhibit 1-10. Summaries of your activities appear under the respective headings.

By default, under Calendar, you can see scheduled appointments for up to five days. Under Tasks, you'll see a summary of all the task items you've created. Under Messages, you'll see the number of unread messages you have (in Inbox), the number of messages you've created but not sent (in Drafts), and the number of sent messages that have not left the computer (in Outbox). You can also click these headings to access the associated folders.

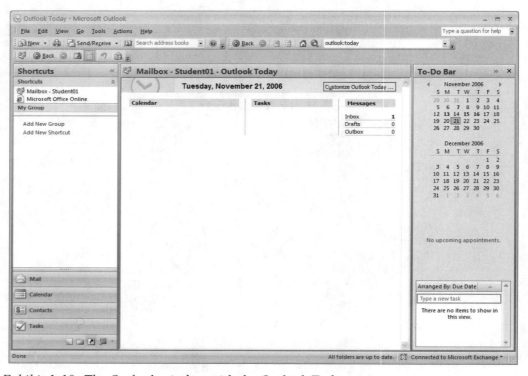

Exhibit 1-10: The Outlook window with the Outlook Today page

Do it!

B-1:   Accessing folders from Outlook Today

Here's how	Here's why
1 Activate Folders view	Click the Folders icon in the Navigation pane.
2 Select the Mailbox – Student \<yy\> folder	(Where \<yy\> is your student number.) The Outlook Today page appears and provides a summary of the day's plan. It displays this summary in three sections: Calendar, Tasks, and Messages.
3 Point to **Messages**	The pointer's shape changes to a hand, and the text is underlined.
Click **Messages**	To open the Mail pane and the Inbox folder. Notice that the messages you received appear in the Folder Contents list.

Customizing Outlook Today

Explanation

You can customize Outlook Today by using the Customize Outlook Today link. This link is located in the upper-right corner of the Outlook Today page.

The following table describes some of the ways in which you can customize Outlook Today.

Option	Description
Startup	Displays the Outlook Today page when Outlook is opened.
Messages	Displays selected folders in the Messages section.
Calendar	Displays the selected number of days from your calendar in the Calendar section.
Tasks	Displays and sorts the selected tasks in the Tasks section.
Styles	Changes the layout or color scheme of the Outlook Today page.

Make your changes to customize Outlook Today, and then click Save Changes. Your customized settings will take effect immediately.

Assigning a home page to an Outlook folder

You can change the default home page for Outlook folders, including Outlook Today. To assign a new home page to the Outlook Today folder:

1 Right-click Outlook Today. A shortcut menu appears.

2 Choose Properties to open the Properties dialog box.

3 Activate the Home Page tab.

4 In the Address box, enter the Web-page address that you want to set as the home page for Outlook Today. You can also click Browse to navigate to the page. (The Restore Defaults button is used to reset the Outlook Today page as the home page.)

5 Click OK.

Do it!

B-2: Customizing Outlook Today

Here's how	Here's why
1 Display the Advanced toolbar	Choose View, Toolbars, Advanced.
2 Click	(The Outlook Today button is on the Advanced toolbar.) The Outlook Today page appears.
3 Click as shown Customize Outlook Today ...	(In the Outlook Today page.) To open the Customize Outlook Today page in the Outlook window. You can customize the Calendar, Tasks, and Messages sections of Outlook Today. You can also change the style of the Outlook Today page.
4 Check **When starting, go directly to Outlook Today**	(The option is in the Startup section.) To specify that you want Outlook Today to be the startup page.
Under Tasks, select **Today's tasks** In my task list, show me: ○ All tasks ● Today's tasks ☑ Include tasks with no due date	To specify that only those tasks you have to perform today should appear in the Tasks list.
From the Show Outlook Today in this style list, select **Standard (one column)** Standard ▼ Standard Standard (two column) Standard (one column) Summer Winter	(You might need to scroll down to view the Show Outlook Today in this style list.) A preview of the selected layout appears under the list.

5 Click **Save Changes**	(This link appears in the upper-right corner of the Customize Outlook Today page.) To save the changes and close the Customize Outlook Today page. Your changes take effect immediately, and the Calendar, Tasks, and Messages headings appear in a single column.
6 Choose **File**, **Exit**	To close Outlook. Next, you'll restart Outlook to verify that the change from the Inbox page to the Outlook Today page is reflected in the startup folder.
7 Start Outlook	(Click Start, and then choose All Programs, Microsoft Office, Microsoft Office Outlook 2007.) The Outlook Today page is now the startup page.
8 Activate Folders	(If necessary.) Click the Folders icon in the Navigation pane.
9 Right-click the **Mailbox – Student <yy>** folder	A shortcut menu appears.
Choose **Properties**	To open the Properties dialog box for your Mailbox. The Mailbox stores all the mail-related folders, such as Inbox, Outbox, and Drafts.
Activate the Home Page tab	The Address box displays the address of the current home page. The option "Show home page by default for this folder" is checked. You'll make the Web page of Outlander Spices the default home page of Outlook Today.
10 Click **Browse**	To open the Find Web Files dialog box.
Navigate to the current unit folder	
Double-click **My Web**	To open the My Web folder.
Select **Index**	If necessary.
Click **OK**	To close the Find Web Files dialog box.
11 Click **OK**	To close the Properties dialog box. Notice that the Outlander Spices Web page appears in the Outlook Today page.
	A message box might appear informing you that certain types of addresses could not be obtained.
Click **OK**	(If necessary.) To close the message box.
Click **Cancel**	(If necessary.) To close the Properties dialog box for your Mailbox.

Topic C: Getting help

Explanation

You can use Outlook's help system to get assistance while you're working. You can access help by using the Type a question for help box or by using the Microsoft Office Outlook Help window.

Type a question for help box

The Type a question for help box is always available on the Outlook menu bar. To access help, type a question in the box and press Enter. The Search Results task pane displays the related help topics. Click any topic to display help for that topic in the Microsoft Outlook Help window.

Do it!

C-1: Using the Type a question for help box

Here's how	Here's why
1 Observe the right side of the menu bar	Type a question for help ⌄
	To view the Type a question for help box.
2 Click the **Type a question for help** box	
Type **Calendar**	
Press ⏎ ENTER	The Microsoft Office Outlook Help window appears on top of the Outlook window. This window displays the help topics related to Calendar.
3 Click a help topic	To open the help topic in the Microsoft Office Outlook Help window. The window displays information on the selected help topic.
Close the Help window	Click the Close button in the upper-right corner of the Help window.
4 Observe the Type a question for help box	The word "Calendar" appears in the box. Your questions will be saved so that you can reuse them in the future.
5 Click the down arrow	(On the Type a question for help box.) To display the list of previous questions. Currently, Calendar is the only available entry.
Press ESC	To hide the list in the Type a question for help box.

Microsoft Office Outlook Help window

Explanation

You can choose Help, Microsoft Office Outlook Help or press F1 to directly open the Microsoft Office Outlook Help window, shown in Exhibit 1-11. From the first Search list, you select where you want to search. You can perform offline or online searches. In the second Search box, you enter the text on which you need help. Click the Go button to perform the search. The results of the search appear in the window.

You can also browse the available help topics. To do so, click the Outlook Home button and then click one of the topics to display it in the window. The Microsoft Office Help window is available in all Office applications.

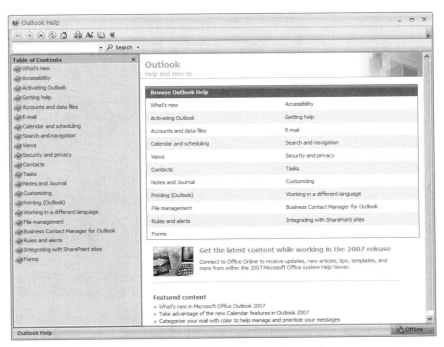

Exhibit 1-11: The Microsoft Office Outlook Help window

Do it!

C-2: Using the Microsoft Office Outlook Help window

Here's how	Here's why
1 Choose **Help, Microsoft Office Outlook Help**	To open the Microsoft Office Outlook Help window. Notice that the insertion point appears in the Search box. You can enter specific words or phrases here.
2 In the Search box, enter **events**	(Type "events" and press Enter.) The help topic appears in the window.
3 Click **Create an all-day event**	The Microsoft Office Outlook Help window displays information on the selected help topic (in this case, Create an all-day event).
Close the Microsoft Office Outlook Help window	Click the Close button in the upper-right corner of the Microsoft Office Outlook Help window.

Unit summary: Getting started

Topic A

In this topic, you learned how to **start Outlook 2007**. You also learned about the **common window elements** that are found in the Outlook 2007 window, such as the title bar, the menu bar, the Standard toolbar, and the status bar. Next, you learned about the elements that are specific to the Outlook 2007 window, such as the **Navigation pane**, the **Folder pane**, the **Reading pane** and the **To-Do bar**. Then you learned how to access the default panes that are available in the Navigation pane, such as Mail, Inbox, Calendar, Contacts, and Tasks. Next, you learned how to access the default Outlook folders by using the Folder list pane. You also learned how to use the Advanced toolbar.

Topic B

In this topic, you learned that **Outlook Today** is a folder that displays your events, appointments, meetings, and tasks planned for the day. You also learned how to **customize** the Calendar, Tasks, and Messages sections of Outlook Today, as well as change the style of the Outlook Today page.

Topic C

In this topic, you learned how to get help by using the **Type a question for help box** and by directly accessing the **Microsoft Office Outlook Help window**.

Independent practice activity

In this activity, you'll customize the Outlook Today page. You'll also use the Microsoft Office Outlook help window to locate information on specific topics.

1 Restore the default home page for the Outlook Today page. To do so, open the Properties dialog box for the Mailbox folder, activate the Home Page tab, click Restore Defaults, and click OK.

2 Customize Outlook's startup so it does not go directly to the Outlook Today page. (*Hint*: In the Outlook Today pane, click Customize Outlook Today.)

3 Customize the Outlook Today page to show the following folders in the Messages section: Deleted Items, Inbox, Junk E-mail, Outbox, and Sent Items.

4 Customize the Outlook Today page to display All tasks.

5 Customize the Outlook Today page to be displayed in the Summer style.

6 Save the changes to Outlook Today.

7 Close Microsoft Office Outlook 2007.

8 Start Microsoft Office Outlook 2007.

9 Use the Type a question for help box to access help on **Notes**.

10 Use the Microsoft Office Outlook Help window to access help on **Contacts**.

11 Close the Microsoft Office Outlook Help window.

Review questions

1 In addition to sending and receiving e-mail messages, what other activities does Outlook help you manage?

2 Which of the following is not an Outlook item?

   A An e-mail message

   B Note

   C Contact

   D Folder

3 Which pane contains the pane-switching buttons that enable you to display the calendar instead of your Inbox?

4 Which default folder helps you keep a record of interactions that you want to remember?

   A Inbox

   B Journal

   C Sent items

   D Drafts

5 Which default folder stores filtered junk e-mail messages?

   A Inbox

   B Deleted Items

   C Junk E-mail

   D Drafts

6 How do you display the Advanced toolbar?

7 Which pane displays the contents of a mail item?

8 What is Outlook Today?

9 What is the To-Do bar?

10 Name at least two ways to get help in Outlook.

Unit 2

E-mail

Unit time: 60 minutes

Complete this unit, and you'll know how to:

A Configure e-mail accounts such as a Microsoft Exchange Server account and an Outlook Anywhere connection, and configure a Hotmail e-mail account and a POP3 e-mail account.

B Use the Inbox to preview and read messages.

C Create and send messages and work with automation and formatting features.

D Reply to messages, forward and resend messages, save a message as a file, and delete and restore messages.

E Preview, open, read, forward, and save file attachments; and compress images in attachments.

Topic A: E-mail accounts

This topic covers the following Microsoft Certified Application Specialist exam objective for Outlook 2007.

#	Objective
5.6.4	**Configure Outlook to be accessible through the Web**
	• Configure RPC over HTTP

Connecting to the Internet

Explanation

E-mail is used to send and receive messages through the Internet. To send and receive e-mail, you first need a way to connect to the Internet. There are several ways you can connect to the Internet:

- Through a local area network (LAN), which might use DSL (Digital Subscriber Line) or cable modems
- Through a traditional dial-up modem connection

You'll also need to use the services of an *Internet Service Provider (ISP)*. ISPs, such as America Online (AOL), MSN, and EarthLink, supply Internet connectivity services to individuals, businesses, and other organizations.

After you have an Internet connection, you'll need to set up an e-mail account. An *e-mail account* contains the information that identifies a user so that the user can send and receive e-mail messages. A user can have more than one e-mail account. To access an e-mail account, a user should have a user name and a password. A *user name* is a unique identifier for every user, and a *password* is a unique identifier that the user enters for security reasons.

Outlook e-mail accounts

Depending on your needs, you might have multiple e-mail accounts that you use for business or personal purposes. You can configure all these accounts in Outlook 2007. When you do so, these accounts are added to your user profile. You can then send and receive messages from Outlook by using any of these accounts.

Outlook sets one account as the default account and uses it to send and receive e-mail. You can also send e-mail from other accounts. To do so, you need to select the account name from the Accounts list at the top of the Message window. This list appears only if you have configured multiple accounts.

There are two basic types of accounts you can configure for an Outlook profile: Microsoft Exchange Server and Internet e-mail. Before you add a new e-mail account to your current Outlook user profile, you need to have the following information:

- The type of account you want to configure, such as Exchange Server, POP3, IMAP4, or HTTP
- Names of the incoming and outgoing mail servers
- Your user name and password, necessary to connect to the server
- Your complete e-mail address, such as "Student01@outlanderspices.com"

Microsoft Exchange Server accounts

Microsoft Exchange Server is a type of mail server used in an intranet. An *intranet* is a network that is based on TCP/IP protocols, that belongs to an organization, and that is accessible only to the organization's members or any other authorized users. The members of an intranet use a Microsoft Exchange Server account to send and receive messages. To do this, each user needs to configure an account in Outlook. Only one Microsoft Exchange Server account can be configured for a profile at a time.

Use the following steps to configure a Microsoft Exchange Server account in Outlook:

1 Verify that the computer is set up to connect to the Microsoft Exchange Server and that the Exchange Server Mailbox has been created.

2 Open Outlook 2007.

3 If this is the first time Outlook 2007 is opened, the Account Configuration, E-mail Accounts screen will appear. Verify that Yes is selected and click Next. If this is a second Outlook account, choose Tools, Account Settings to open the Account Settings dialog box, as shown in Exhibit 2-1. Then, activate the E-mail tab, and then click New.

4 On the Add New E-mail Account, Choose E-mail Service screen, verify that Microsoft Exchange, POP3, IMAP, or HTTP is selected, as shown in Exhibit 2-2, and then click Next.

5 On the Account Basics screen, enter the user name and e-mail address. Outlook will automatically search for the Exchange Server and your mailbox. If the automatic detection succeeds, click Finish. If automatic detection fails, check Manually configure server settings and enter the name of the Exchange Server, the user name, and the e-mail address. If the manual settings fail, check your connection settings and Exchange Server mailbox configuration.

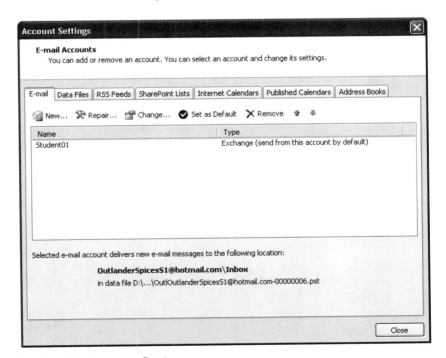

Exhibit 2-1: Account Settings

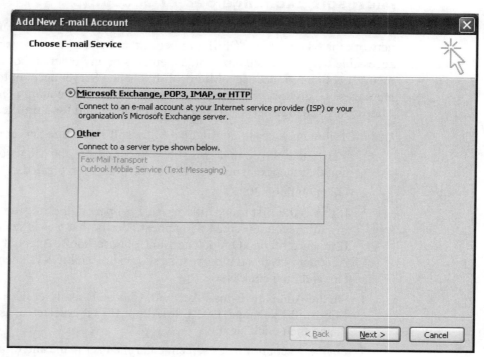

Exhibit 2-2: E-mail services

Enable an Outlook Anywhere connection

If you work from a remote site and need to access an Exchange Server when you are outside of your company's firewall, you can use Outlook Anywhere as an alternative to a VPN (virtual private network) connection. An Outlook Anywhere connection allows you to use Outlook just as you normally would at your company and does not require any additional connections or hardware. Outlook connects to the Exchange Server through the Internet by using RPC (remote procedure call) over HTTP.

To use Outlook Anywhere, you must meet the following requirements:

- Your computer must be running Windows XP with SP2 or later.
- The Exchange Server must be running Exchange Server 2003 or Microsoft Exchange 2007 on Windows Server 2003.
- Your Exchange Server administrator must configure the server to permit connections via HTTP.

Do it!   **A-1: Configuring an Outlook Anywhere connection**

Here's how	Here's why
1 Choose **Tools**, **Account Settings...**	(You might need to click the chevron on the Tools menu.) To open the Account Settings dialog box.
2 On the E-mail tab, select your Exchange Server account	
3 Click **Change**	To change the settings for your Exchange Server account.
4 Click **More Settings**	To open the Microsoft Exchange dialog box.
5 Activate the Connection tab	
6 Under Outlook Anywhere, check **Connect to Microsoft Exchange using HTTP**	To activate an Outlook Anywhere connection.
Click **Exchange Proxy Settings**	To view the Microsoft Exchange Proxy Settings dialog box. Notice the connection settings and authentication settings required.
Click **Cancel**	To close the dialog box without keeping any changes.
Clear **Connect to Microsoft Exchange using HTTP**	To deactivate the Outlook Anywhere connection.
Click **Cancel** twice	To close the dialog boxes without keeping any changes.
7 Click **Close**	To close the Account Settings dialog box.

Internet e-mail accounts

Explanation

An Internet e-mail account can use one of the following protocols:

- Hypertext Transfer Protocol (HTTP)
- Post Office Protocol 3 (POP3)
- Internet Message Access Protocol (IMAP)

A *protocol* is a set of rules or standards designed to help computers communicate with each other through a network or on the Internet. For example, the Hotmail account uses HTTP, which is used for communicating over the Internet. POP3 and IMAP are both used to retrieve e-mail messages from a mail server, but IMAP has some additional features. For example, with IMAP, you can search through e-mail messages for keywords while the messages are still on the mail server. You can then choose which messages are to be downloaded to your machine. You can configure several Internet e-mail accounts for a profile.

Configuring an HTTP account

One account that uses HTTP is a Hotmail account. You can access a Hotmail account by logging on to it. For this, you need to have a user name and a password. *Logging on* is the process of gaining access to an e-mail account by entering the correct user name and password, as shown in Exhibit 2-3.

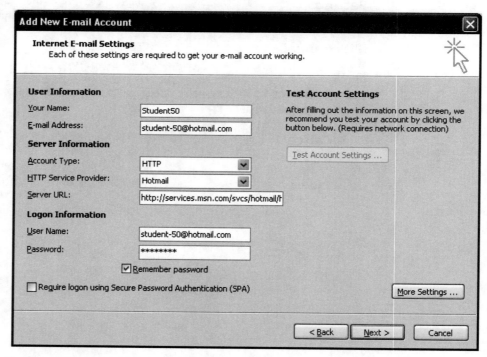

Exhibit 2-3: The Add New E-mail Account dialog box

Do it!   **A-2: Configuring a Hotmail account**

Here's how	Here's why
1 Choose **Tools, Account Settings...**	(You might need to click the chevron on the Tools menu.) To open the Account Settings dialog box.
2 On the E-mail tab, click **New**	To open the Add New E-mail Account dialog box. You'll configure a new e-mail account in Outlook.
3 Verify **Microsoft Exchange, POP3, IMAP, or HTTP** is selected Click **Next**	
4 Check **Manually configure server settings or additional server types** Click **Next**	(At the bottom of the dialog box.) To manually configure the Hotmail account.
5 Verify that Internet E-mail is selected and click **Next**	
6 In the Your Name box, enter your name Press ⌐TAB⌐	To move the insertion point to the E-mail Address box.
7 In the E-mail Address box, enter your Hotmail e-mail address Press ⌐TAB⌐	
8 From the Account type list, select **HTTP** From the HTTP Service Provider list, select **Hotmail**	If necessary.
9 In the Server URL box, enter **http://services.msn.com/svcs/hotmail/httpmail.asp**	If necessary.
10 In the User Name box, enter your Hotmail e-mail address	

11 In the Password box, enter your password	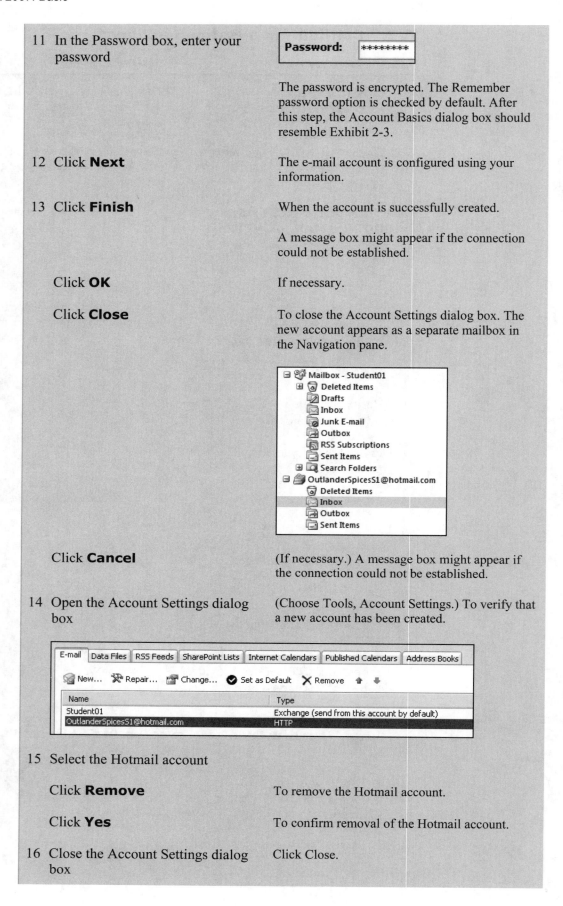**Password:** ********
	The password is encrypted. The Remember password option is checked by default. After this step, the Account Basics dialog box should resemble Exhibit 2-3.
12 Click **Next**	The e-mail account is configured using your information.
13 Click **Finish**	When the account is successfully created.
	A message box might appear if the connection could not be established.
Click **OK**	If necessary.
Click **Close**	To close the Account Settings dialog box. The new account appears as a separate mailbox in the Navigation pane.

	⊟ 📇 Mailbox - Student01
	  ⊞ Deleted Items
	  Drafts
	  Inbox
	  Junk E-mail
	  Outbox
	  RSS Subscriptions
	  Sent Items
	  ⊞ Search Folders
	⊟ OutlanderSpicesS1@hotmail.com
	  Deleted Items
	  Inbox
	  Outbox
	  Sent Items

Click **Cancel**	(If necessary.) A message box might appear if the connection could not be established.
14 Open the Account Settings dialog box	(Choose Tools, Account Settings.) To verify that a new account has been created.

E-mail | Data Files | RSS Feeds | SharePoint Lists | Internet Calendars | Published Calendars | Address Books

New...   Repair...   Change...   Set as Default   X Remove   ⬆   ⬇

Name	Type
Student01	Exchange (send from this account by default)
OutlanderSpicesS1@hotmail.com	HTTP

15 Select the Hotmail account	
Click **Remove**	To remove the Hotmail account.
Click **Yes**	To confirm removal of the Hotmail account.
16 Close the Account Settings dialog box	Click Close.

POP3 or IMAP accounts

Explanation

If you are connected to the Internet through an ISP, you might need to manually set up an Internet e-mail account that uses either POP3 or IMAP as the protocol. ISPs use either a POP3 server or an IMAP server.

To have access to the Internet, you'll need to register with an ISP. After you register with an ISP, you'll get a user name, a password, and a method to connect to the Internet. The manual configuration for a typical POP3 account is shown in Exhibit 2-4.

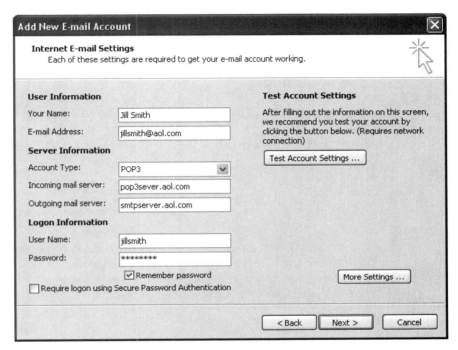

Exhibit 2-4: Internet E-mail Settings

Do it!

A-3: Configuring a POP3 account

Here's how	Here's why
1 Open the Account Settings dialog box	Choose Tools, Account Settings.
2 Under E-mail, click **New**	You'll manually configure a new e-mail account in Outlook.
3 Click **Next**	Verify that Microsoft Exchange, POP3, IMAP, or HTTP is selected.
Check **Manually configure server settings**	Notice that the Account Basics screen becomes inactive.
Click **Next**	The Choose E-mail Service screen appears.
4 Select **Internet E-mail**	To configure a POP3, IMAP, Hotmail, or other ISP account.
Click **Next**	**Internet E-mail Settings** Each of these settings are required to get your e-mail account working.
	An Internet E-mail Settings tip informs you that these settings are necessary to get your e-mail account working.
5 In the Your Name box, type your name	
Press (TAB)	
In the E-mail Address box, type your e-mail address	
Press (TAB)	The user name appears in the User Name box.
6 From the Account Type list, select **POP3**	If necessary.
7 In the Incoming mail server box, enter the incoming mail server's address	
In the Outgoing mail server box, enter the outgoing mail server's address	
8 In the Password box, enter your password	The password is encrypted. Notice that the Remember password option is checked by default.
	After this step, the Add New E-mail Account dialog box should resemble Exhibit 2-4.

9	Click **Next**	A message appears, indicating that you have successfully entered all the information necessary to set up your account.
	Click **Finish**	To return to the Account Settings dialog box. Verify that a new e-mail account has been created. The name of the POP3 server appears in the Account Settings dialog box.
10	Close the Account Settings dialog box	Click Close.

Topic B: Reading e-mail messages

This topic covers the following Microsoft Certified Application Specialist exam objective for Outlook 2007.

#	Objective
1.7.2	**Automatically preview messages**

The Inbox

Explanation

You can use Outlook to view, reply to, and forward messages you receive. In addition, when you receive an e-mail message, you can save the message itself as a file or you can forward it to others. You can also delete e-mail messages and restore deleted messages.

By default, all the messages you receive are stored in the *Inbox* folder. This is one of the most frequently used folders in Outlook. You can read a message stored in the Inbox. You can also create a new message and send it. If you want to, you can reply to a message. The Folder pane displays the Folder Contents list. The Reading pane is used to view messages.

Message header

The header of an e-mail message appears in the Folder Contents list, and has the following information:

- **From** — Tells you the name of the sender of the message.
- **Subject** — Indicates the subject of the message, if any. This column helps you identify the content of the message.
- **Received** — Contains the date and time when the message was received.

The header information also contains an icon. The following table describes the icons you might see beside messages in the Folder Contents list:

Icon	Description
✉	A new and unread message.
✉	A message that's been read.
✉	A message that's been read and replied to.
✉	A message that's been read and forwarded.
📎	A message with a file attachment.
🚩	A flagged message.

Do it!　　　**B-1:   Exploring the Inbox**

Here's how	Here's why
1 Select **Inbox**	(In the Favorite Folders list.) To view your Outlook Inbox.
2 Observe the Standard toolbar	It has mail-specific buttons.
3 View the status bar	It shows the total number of messages in the Inbox.
4 Examine the header information of the first message	
	It shows the name of the sender (Instructor) and the subject of the message (Welcome to Outlook 2007). The header also shows an icon of an open envelope to the left of the sender's name; this icon tells you that this message has been read.
5 Observe the Reading pane	You cannot edit messages in the Reading Pane. The Reading Pane shows the content of the message that is selected in the Folder Contents list.

Previewing and reading messages

Explanation
All new messages are delivered to the Inbox. Messages that have not been read appear in bold with a closed-envelope icon. Messages that have been read appear in regular text with an open-envelope icon.

Previewing messages

There are two ways to preview messages. You can either preview the first three lines of messages in the Folder Contents list or preview the content of a message in the Reading pane. To preview the first three lines of messages, choose View, AutoPreview. To view items in the Reading pane, choose View, Reading Pane and then choose Right or Bottom.

Reading messages

To read a message, select the message you want to read in the Folder Contents list. You can either read the message in the Reading pane or open it in a Message window by double-clicking it.

As shown in Exhibit 2-5, a Message window contains four sections: the Office button and Quick Access toolbar, the Ribbon, the message header, and the message body.

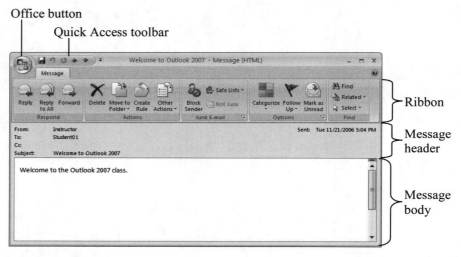

Exhibit 2-5: A received message

Working with the Office button and Quick Access toolbar

The Office button displays a list of commonly used file commands, such as New Message, Save As, Delete, and Print. The Quick Access toolbar contains buttons for frequently used commands: by default, Save, Undo, Repeat/Redo, Print (Fax), Previous Item, and Next Item are available. You can customize it to include additional commands.

Working with the Ribbon

The Ribbon is made up of controls such as buttons, lists, and galleries, which are organized into groups. In addition, the Ribbon can contain multiple tabs, which you activate to view a different set of groups and items. The tabs and groups available on the Ribbon depend on the opened window, active folder, or selected object. The Ribbon for a new Message window is shown in Exhibit 2-6.

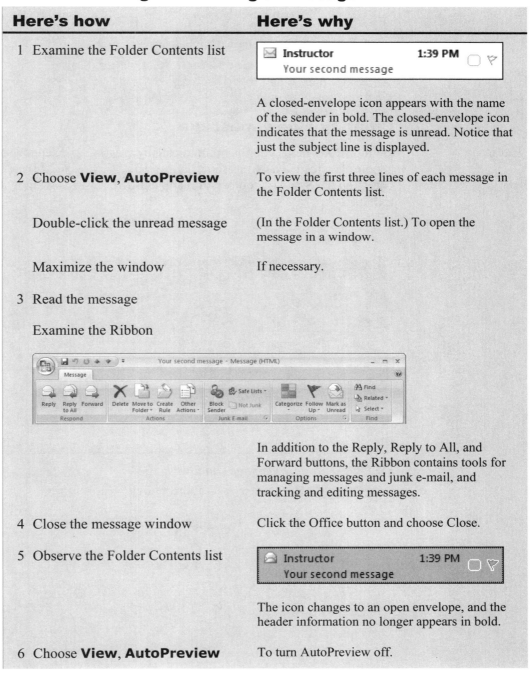

Exhibit 2-6: The Ribbon for a new message

Do it!

B-2:   Previewing and reading a message

Here's how	Here's why
1 Examine the Folder Contents list	✉ **Instructor** 1:39 PM ☐ ▽ Your second message
	A closed-envelope icon appears with the name of the sender in bold. The closed-envelope icon indicates that the message is unread. Notice that just the subject line is displayed.
2 Choose **View**, **AutoPreview**	To view the first three lines of each message in the Folder Contents list.
Double-click the unread message	(In the Folder Contents list.) To open the message in a window.
Maximize the window	If necessary.
3 Read the message	
Examine the Ribbon	
	In addition to the Reply, Reply to All, and Forward buttons, the Ribbon contains tools for managing messages and junk e-mail, and tracking and editing messages.
4 Close the message window	Click the Office button and choose Close.
5 Observe the Folder Contents list	✉ Instructor 1:39 PM ☐ ▽ Your second message
	The icon changes to an open envelope, and the header information no longer appears in bold.
6 Choose **View**, **AutoPreview**	To turn AutoPreview off.

Topic C: Creating and sending e-mail messages

This topic covers the following Microsoft Certified Application Specialist exam objectives for Outlook 2007.

#	Objective
1.1.1	**Send messages to multiple recipients**
	• Carbon copy recipients
	• Blind carbon copy recipients
5.6.3	**Select the default format for messages**
	• Set default message format (HTML, Rich Text, Text)

Creating a new message

Explanation

Outlook 2007 helps you to communicate by creating and sending e-mail messages to people. To create a new message, choose File, New, Mail Message, or click the New button on the Standard toolbar. A blank untitled Message window opens, as shown in Exhibit 2-7.

Ribbon

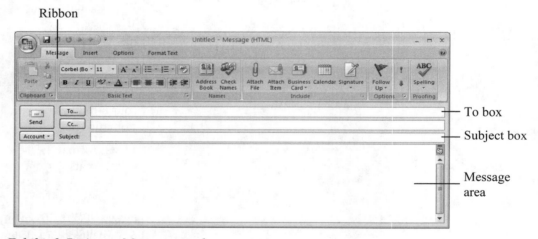

Exhibit 2-7: A new Message window

The following table describes the components of a new Message window.

Component	Description
To box	Contains the e-mail addresses of all the people (recipients) to whom you want to send the message. To send a message to multiple recipients, separate the e-mail addresses with semicolons.
Cc box	Contains the e-mail addresses of all the people to whom you want to send a copy of the message.
Subject box	Contains a word or phrase that describes the message.
Message area	Contains the contents of the message.
Ribbon	Contains buttons for frequently used actions, such as sending messages, attaching files, and flagging messages. Also, contains buttons that help you apply styles, fonts, and other character formats to your message text.

The Bcc box

By default, a new message window does not include a Bcc box for specifying recipients to whom you want to secretly send a copy of the e-mail message. Any recipients whose e-mail addresses you specify in the Bcc box will receive a copy of the message, but their names won't appear to any other recipients who receive the e-mail message.

To add the Bcc box to a message you're composing, activate the Options tab on the Ribbon, and in the Fields group, click Show Bcc.

Selecting the message format

By default, Outlook uses Word as the e-mail editor for new messages. To use Word as the e-mail editor, Word must be installed on your machine and it must be the same version as Outlook. When you use Word as your e-mail editor, you can take advantage of Word features such as AutoCorrect and automatic spelling and grammar checking.

By default, new messages are composed in HTML format. HTML formatting in a message lets you apply character and paragraph formats to your message text. You can also change the formatting of either all your messages or a single message to plain text or Rich Text. When you create a plain text message, you cannot use the formatting tools on the Ribbon. Rich Text formatting is compatible only with Outlook and Exchange. If you use Rich Text to send a message to someone using an e-mail client other than Outlook, the formatting will be lost.

To change the message format for a single message, open a new message and click the Options tab. Then click Plain Text or Rich Text in the Format group on the Ribbon. Click the Message tab to continue composing your message.

To change the default message format for all messages, choose Tools, Options. Activate the Mail Format tab. Under Message format, select the new default formatting from the list and click OK.

Sending messages

After creating a message, you need to send it. You do this by clicking the Send button on the Ribbon or by pressing Ctrl+Enter.

Whenever you are online and receive a new message, a Desktop Alert appears in the notification area on the Taskbar, indicating that you have received a new message.

C-1: Creating and sending a message

Here's how	Here's why
1 Choose **Tools**, **Options...**	You'll reset the default message format to plain text.
Activate the Mail Format tab	Notice the default message format is HTML.
Select **Plain Text**	Under Message format, from the Compose in this message format list.
Click **OK**	
2 Verify that the Inbox is active	
3 Click **New** as shown	(On the Standard toolbar.) To open a new message. Notice that the formatting tools in the Basic Text group on the Ribbon are not available because the message format is plain text.
4 In the To box, enter **Student<xx>**	In place of <xx>, enter your partner's number.
5 Press ⟨TAB⟩	To move the insertion point to the Cc box. You can enter another e-mail address here to send a copy of the message to that person.
6 In the Cc box, enter your instructor's e-mail address	You'll also send a blind carbon copy of the message to another student. However, the Bcc box doesn't appear by default.
7 Activate the Options tab	
Click **Show Bcc**	(In the Fields group.) To display the Bcc box.
8 In the Bcc box, enter the address of another student	This student will receive a copy of the e-mail, but his or her name won't appear in the copies received by other recipients.
9 In the Subject box, enter **Greetings Student<xx>**	In place of <xx>, enter your partner's number.
10 Click **Send**	To send the message to your partner.
11 Click **Send/Receive**	(On the Standard toolbar.) A new message from your partner appears in the Folder Contents list.
12 Change the default message format back to HTML	Choose Tools, Options. Activate the Mail Format tab. Under Message format, select HTML and click OK.

Automation features

Explanation

When you manually enter names in the To or Cc boxes, Outlook automatically checks your address books for the names. *Address books* contains the names of people with whom you frequently communicate. If the entered name matches an address book entry, then the name is underlined with a solid black line. If multiple matching names are found, the name is underlined with a red, wavy line. This name-checking feature is turned on by default. You can also manually check names by clicking the Check Names button on the Ribbon.

As an e-mail editor, Word provides several features, such as smart tags, AutoCorrect, AutoComplete, and spelling and grammar checking. Additionally, if you begin to type an e-mail address that you've previously used, the e-mail editor will automatically try to complete the name. If there are multiple matches, the e-mail editor will provide a list of possible names. For example, if you type "John," the e-mail editor might suggest "John Smith" and "John Williams." You can either continue typing the name or select a name from the shortcut menu. You can also press Ctrl+K to select the name after typing a few characters in the To box.

C-2: Working with automation features

Here's how	Here's why
1 Open a new Message window	Click New on the Standard toolbar.
2 In the To box, enter **S**	A list appears indicating all the names starting with S.
Press ⬇ to select your e-mail partner	If necessary.
Press TAB	Outlook automatically completes the name based on the e-mail addresses that you've used earlier. Notice that Student<##> is entered in the box automatically.
In the Subject box, enter **Student<xx>: Welcome to the class on Outlook 2007**	Press Tab twice to position the insertion point in the Subject box. In place of <xx>, enter your partner's number.
3 Press TAB	To move the insertion point into the message area.
In the message area, type **Dear Student<xx>,**	In place of <xx>, enter your partner's number.
Press ↵ ENTER twice	To create a blank line.
4 Type **today**	
Press SPACEBAR	Notice that the "today" you typed is converted to "Today" because of the Word's AutoCorrect feature.
5 Type **is**	
Type the first four letters of today's weekday	Dear Student02, Monday (Press ENTER to Insert) Today is Mond
	For example, type "Mond" if today is Monday.
Press ↵ ENTER	To complete the word automatically.
6 Type **, the first day for the class on Outlook 2007.**	To complete the sentence.
7 Create a blank line	Press Enter twice.

8 Type **Jhn Wright**

Jhn

The word Jhn appears underlined with a red wavy line. This indicates that the spelling is wrong.

Right-click **Jhn**

| John |
| Jan |
| Jon |
| Johns |

A shortcut menu and the Mini toolbar appear. The shortcut menu displays the possible corrections for the misspelled word.

Choose **John**

(From the shortcut menu.) To correct the misspelled word.

9 Press (END)

To move the insertion point to the end of the line.

Press (↵ ENTER)

To move to the next line.

10 Type **For**

Press (SPACEBAR)

11 Type **Outlander Spices**

12 Click **Send**

To send the message to your partner.

13 Click **Send/Receive**

To receive a message from your partner.

Formatting messages

Explanation

When you create or reply to a message, you might want to emphasize some important text. You can emphasize important text by changing its color, size, or font. You can also underline or italicize text to emphasize it. You use the Basic Text group on the Ribbon, shown in Exhibit 2-8, to format the text in a message.

Exhibit 2-8: A new Message window Ribbon

For additional styles and formatting options, activate the Format Text tab, shown in Exhibit 2-9.

Exhibit 2-9: The Format Text tab

You can also use the Mini toolbar to format the text in a message. To display the Mini toolbar, select the text you want to format and the Mini toolbar appears above the selected text, as shown in Exhibit 2-10. If you point away from the selected text, the Mini toolbar will disappear.

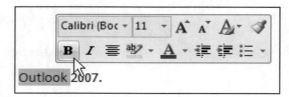

Exhibit 2-10: The Mini toolbar

Do it!

C-3: Formatting a message

Here's how	Here's why
1 Open a new Message window	Click New.
2 In the To box, enter the name of your partner	To address the message to your partner.
In the Subject box, enter **<xx>: Venue for the class**	In place of <xx>, enter your partner's number.
Press (TAB)	To move the insertion point into the message area.
In the message area, type as shown	Dear Student02, The venue for the class is specified below. Venu: Outlander Spices, 1170 Blackhorse Avenue, Texas
3 Select as shown	The venue for the class is specified below. You'll format this text.
4 From the Font Size list, select **12**	The Font Size list is in the Basic Text group on the Ribbon.
From the Font list, select **Arial Black**	The Font list is in the Basic Text group on the Message tab.
Deselect the text	(Click anywhere in the message area.) The font and font size of the message text have changed.
5 Select **Outlander Spices**	(This text is in the message area.) You'll change the format for this text to make it different from the rest of the text.
Click **B**	(The Bold button is in the Basic Text group on the Message tab.) To make the selected text bold.
6 Click ▣ Copy	(The Copy button is in the Clipboard group on the Message tab.) To copy the selected text. You'll paste it later.
7 Click **U**	(The Underline button is in the Basic Text group on the Message tab.) To underline the selected text.
Deselect the text	Notice that the text format has changed.
Place the insertion point as shown	Texas

8 Press ⏎ ENTER

   Type **Time:**

   Press SPACEBAR

   Type **10:30 AM tomorrow**   To specify the time of the class.

9 Create a blank line

   Type **For**

   Press SPACEBAR

10 Click as shown

(The Paste button is in the Clipboard group on the Message tab.) To paste the text copied earlier. The Paste Options button appears after the copied text.

11 Click as shown

A list appears.

   Observe the list

You can paste the copied text with its original formatting, with the destination formatting, or as simple text without any formatting.

   Choose **Keep Text Only**

The text appears without its original formatting.

12 Press ⏎ ENTER   To move to the next line.

   Type your user name   (To complete the message.) The user name represents your name in the class.

                                      Next, you'll format text by using the Mini toolbar.

13 Select as shown, and keep the
pointer over the selected text

> Time: 10:30 AM tomorrow

To display the Mini toolbar. You'll make this
text bold.

Click as shown

> Calibri (Boc ▾ 11 ▾ A˄ A˅ A͟▾ ⬩
> **B** *I* ≡ ᵃᵇⁱ ▾ **A** ▾ ⁝≡ ⁝≡ ⁝≡ ▾
> Time: 10:30 AM tomorrow

Press [END]

To deselect the text.

Checking spelling and grammar in messages

Explanation   By default, Microsoft Word checks spelling and grammar automatically as you type. If you misspell a word, a wavy red line appears under the word. If Word finds a grammatical problem, a wavy green line appears under the word or words. If you mistype a word and the result is not a misspelling (for example, "form" instead of "from") then the spelling checker will not flag the word.

You can also postpone proofing your message until after you finish writing it. To start checking the spelling, either press F7 or click the Spelling button in the Proofing group on the Ribbon to open the Spelling and Grammar: English (U.S.) dialog box, shown in Exhibit 2-11.

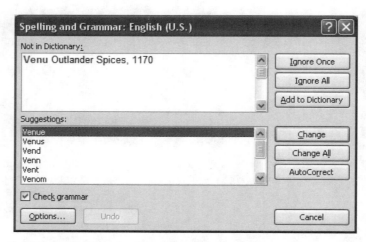

Exhibit 2-11: The Spelling and Grammar: English (U.S.) dialog box

The Not in Dictionary box in the Spelling and Grammar: English (U.S.) dialog box displays words that are not in the Word dictionary. You can choose a suggested spelling from the Suggestions list, and click Change to change a single occurrence of the misspelled word or click Change All to change all occurrences of that word. You can also click Ignore Once to ignore one instance or click Ignore All to ignore all instances of a specific word. In addition, you can clear the Check grammar option if you don't want to check for grammar mistakes.

Do it!   **C-4:   Checking a message's spelling**

Here's how	**Here's why**
1 Click as shown	ABC ✓ Spelling ▾ Proofing
	(In the Proofing group, on the Ribbon.) To open the Spelling and Grammar: English (U.S.) dialog box. This dialog box opens only when there is an incorrect word in the message.
2 Observe the Spelling and Grammar English (U.S.) dialog box	It displays the incorrect word (Venu) in red and prompts you to correct it by selecting a word from the Suggestions list.
From the Suggestions list, select **Venue**	(If necessary.) This is the correct spelling of the word "Venue."
3 Click **Change**	A message box appears, informing you that the spelling and grammar check is complete.
Click **OK**	To close the message box. Notice that "Venu" has changed to "Venue."
4 Send the message	
5 Check for new messages	Click Send/Receive.
6 Select the message with the subject <yy>: Venue for the class	(Click the message in the Inbox.) The contents of the message appear in the Reading pane.

Topic D: Working with messages

This topic covers the following Microsoft Certified Application Specialist exam objectives for Outlook 2007.

#	Objective
1.1.2	**Reply to a message**
	• Reply to all recipients of a message
	• Reply only to the sender of a message
1.1.3	**Resend a message**
	• Open the sent items, select a message, change recipients, and resend the message
1.1.4	**Forward a message**
5.3.4	**Empty the Deleted Mail and Sent Items folders**
	• Permanently delete
	• Set the auto empty options for the deleted items folder

Replying to messages

Explanation

When you open a received message, Outlook provides two reply buttons in the Respond group on the Ribbon:

- Reply: Creates a return message addressed only to the sender.
- Reply to All: Creates a return message addressed to the sender and everyone else who received a carbon copy of the original message.

Reply messages, by default, contain the original message text. This is useful when you need to refer to the original message. Also, when you type any text in the reply Message window, the text appears in blue so you can distinguish between your reply and the original message text.

To send a reply:

1 Open the message to which you want to reply.
2 Click Reply. This opens the reply Message window with the name of the original sender in the To box. The reply message uses the subject of the original message with RE: added as a prefix.
3 Type your reply in the message area.
4 Click Send to send the message.

Do it!   **D-1:   Replying to a message**

Here's how	Here's why
1 Select the message with the subject Student<yy>: Welcome to the class on Outlook 2007	(Click the message in your Inbox, where <yy> is your number.) You'll reply to this message.
2 Click **Reply**	To open a reply Message window and compose a reply.
Observe the reply Message window	To... Student02; Cc... Subject: RE: Student01: Welcome to the class on Outlook 2007 The To box contains the name of the sender of the message. The Subject box displays the same subject with RE: added as a prefix.
3 Verify that the insertion point is in the first line of the message area	You'll type your reply here.
4 Type **Thank you**	
Press ⏎ ENTER	Notice that the message text is blue.
5 Move to the next line	Press Enter.
Type your name	
6 Send the message	Click Send.
7 Observe the message in the Reading pane	You replied on 7/6/2006 11:45 AM. This area is called the InfoBar. It indicates the action taken on the message, along with the date and time. In this case, the action was a reply to a message.
8 Observe the Folder Contents list	Student02 11:44 AM Student01: Welcome to the class... The original message has an icon showing that you have replied to the message.
9 Activate the Folder list	Click the Folder List icon in the Navigation pane.
Click **Sent Items**	(Sent Items is in the Folder List pane.) To open the Sent Items folder. The reply message that you sent appears as an item. Any message that you send will be stored in this folder.

10	Click **Send/Receive**	
	Activate the Inbox	To view your partner's reply.
		Next, you'll use the Reply to All option.
11	Select the message with the subject Greetings Student<yy>	You'll send a reply to the sender along with anyone who received a Cc.
12	Click **Reply to All**	To open a reply Message window and compose a reply.
13	Observe the Reply message window	The To box contains the name of the sender of the message, and the Cc box contains the name of the person who received a copy of the original message. The Subject box displays the same subject with RE: added as a prefix.
14	Type **Hello!**	In the message area.
15	Click **Send**	To send the reply to the sender and the person who was copied on the original message.

Forwarding messages

Explanation

When you receive a message that other people need to know about, you can forward it to them. To forward a message:

1   Open or select the message.
2   Click Forward.
3   Enter the recipient's name in the To box.
4   Click Send.

Do it!

D-2:   Forwarding a message

Here's how	Here's why
1 Select the message with the subject <yy>: Venue for the class	From the Inbox Folder Contents list.
2 Click [🖃 Forward]	(The Forward button is on the Standard toolbar.) The message opens in a new Message window, containing the original message. The subject of the message is the original subject with the prefix FW: added.
3 In the To box, enter another user name	To forward the message to the specified user.
4 In the message area, type **I thought you might find this useful.**	Notice that the text you typed appears in blue.
5 Send the message	
6 Open the Sent Items folder	(Click Sent Items in the Mail pane.) The message that you forwarded appears in the Sent Items Folder Contents list.

Resend messages

Explanation

At times, you might send a message, and later decide to resend the same message to a different recipient. Rather than retyping the identical message, you can resend the original message.

To resend a message to a different recipient:

1 In the Folder List pane, click Sent Items to display the e-mail messages you've sent.

2 Double-click the message you want to resend. A message window appears, displaying the message.

3 On the Message tab, in the Actions group, click Other Actions and choose Resend This Message.

4 In the To box, delete the e-mail address and replace it with the address to which you want to resend the message.

5 Click Send.

Do it!

D-3: Resending a message

Here's how	Here's why
1 Verify that the Sent Items folder is open	You'll resend a message to another student.
2 Double-click the message named <xx>: Venue for the class	To open the message in a message window. You sent this message to your partner earlier.
3 Click **Other Actions** and choose **Resend This Message...**	To open a new message window.
4 In the To box, select the address and press (DELETE)	To delete the address of your partner to whom you sent this message earlier.
5 In the To box, enter another student's e-mail address	
6 Edit the Subject box to reflect the new student's number	
7 Click **Send**	To resend the message to the other student.
8 Close the Message window	

Saving messages

You might want to store an important message as a separate file for future reference. To save a message as a file:

1 Open the message.
2 Click the Office button and click Save As to open the Save As dialog box.
3 In the Save As dialog box, specify the name and location of the file.
4 From the Save as type list, select the type of the file you want to use for the file (such as HTML or Text Only).
5 Click Save.

D-4:   Saving a message as a file

Here's how	Here's why
1 Open the message with the subject <yy>: Venue for the class	(In the Inbox folder.) Double-click the message to open it.
2 Click	
Click **Save As**	To open the Save As dialog box and specify where you want to save the copy of the message.
Navigate to the current unit folder	If necessary.
3 Edit the File name box to read **My venue**	To specify the file name.
In the Save as type list, verify that HTML is selected	To specify that the message should be saved as an HTML file.
Click **Save**	To save the file and close the Save As dialog box.
4 Open the Save As dialog box	(Click the Office button and choose Save As, Save As.) Notice that My venue is visible in the current unit folder.
Click **Cancel**	To close the Save As dialog box.
5 Close the Message window	

Deleting and restoring messages

Explanation

You can delete messages that you don't need any longer. To delete a message, you can select it and click the Delete button on the Standard toolbar. You can also choose Edit, Delete. The deleted message is stored in the Deleted Items folder and remains there until you empty the Deleted Items folder.

To empty the Deleted Items folder and permanently delete the items in that folder, select the folder and choose Tools, Empty "Deleted Items" Folder.

To delete the items in your Deleted Items folder when you close Outlook, choose Tools, Options. Activate the Other tab and check Empty the Deleted Items folder upon exiting. Click OK.

Sometimes, you might need to refer to a deleted message. If the message is still in your Deleted Items folder, you can restore the message by dragging it from the Deleted Items folder to the Inbox.

If you have already emptied the Deleted Items folder, and you're using a Microsoft Exchange server account, you can try to recover a deleted message. To do so, choose Tools, Recover Deleted Items. Select the messages you want to recover and click Recover Selected Items. The messages will appear in the Deleted Items folder.

Do it!   ### D-5:   Deleting and restoring a message

Here's how	Here's why
1 Open the Inbox folder	Click Inbox in the Mail pane.
2 Select the message with the subject Student <yy>: Welcome to the class on Outlook 2007	You'll delete this message.
3 Click ✕	(The Delete button is on the Standard toolbar.) To delete the message. The message is removed from the Folder Contents list.
4 Open the Deleted Items folder	(Click Deleted Items in the Mail pane.) This folder stores all the deleted messages. Notice that the deleted message appears in this folder.
Choose **Tools, Empty "Deleted Items" Folder**	To remove the message from the Deleted Items folder. A dialog box appears, prompting you to confirm the deletion.
Click **Yes**	To confirm the deletion.
5 Choose **Tools, Recover Deleted Items**	To recover the message.
Select the message that has the subject Student <yy>: Welcome to the class on Outlook 2007	
Click 📩	Notice the message appears in the Deleted Items folder again.
6 Drag the message to Inbox	(Select the message, if necessary) To restore the deleted message.
7 Open the Inbox folder	The message that has the "Welcome to the class on Outlook 2007" subject has been restored.
8 Choose **Tools, Options...**	You'll configure Outlook to automatically delete items from your Deleted Items folder when you close Outlook.
Activate the Other tab	
Check **Empty the Deleted Items folder upon exiting**	
Click **OK**	

Topic E: Attachments

This topic covers the following Microsoft Certified Application Specialist exam objectives for Outlook 2007.

#	Objective
1.1.4	**Forward a message** • Forward a message with an attachment
1.3.1	**Attach files and items to a message** • Attach a file to a message • Compress large pictures after adding as an attachment
1.3.2	**Preview a message attachment in Outlook**
1.3.3	**Save attachments to a specific location**
1.3.4	**Open a message attachment**

Attaching files

Explanation

In addition to sending a standard e-mail message, you can add an attachment to the message. When you receive an e-mail message that includes an attachment, you can preview or save the attachment. You can also forward the attachment to others.

Attach a file to a new message

You can attach any type of file to an e-mail message as a way of sending the file to the e-mail recipient. For example, you can send Word, graphic, sound, and movie files as attachments. You can attach a single file or multiple files to a message. The Attach box displays the name and size of the attachment.

To attach a file:

1   Create a new message.
2   Click the Attach File button in the Include group on the Ribbon.
3   Select the file you want to insert.
4   Click Insert. The Attach box, with the attached file, appears under the Subject box.

By default, Outlook blocks potentially unsafe attachments, such as EXE and VBS files, which can contain viruses. If you attach a file with an extension that might be blocked by Outlook, you will be prompted if you want to send a potentially unsafe attachment or not. If you send the attachment anyway, it might be blocked by the recipient's Outlook or antivirus software.

Forward a message that contains an attachment

You can forward a message that contains an attachment by opening the message and clicking Forward. By default, the file is attached to the message. Address the message and click Send.

You can also forward a message and add an attachment. To do so,

1 Open the message you want to forward.
2 Click the Forward button in the Respond group on the Ribbon.
3 Click the Attach File button in the Include group on the Ribbon.
4 Select the file you want to insert.
5 Click Insert. The Attach box, with the attached file, appears under the Subject box.

Do it!

E-1: Sending and forwarding attachments

Here's how	Here's why
1 Open a new Message window	
Address the message to your partner	In the To box, type your partner's e-mail address.
Enter the subject as **<xx>: Sales Report**	In the Subject box. In place of <xx>, enter your partner's number.
2 In the message area, type **I am sending the West Coast sales report.**	
3 Click as shown	

(The Attach File button is in the Include group on the Ribbon.) To open the Insert File dialog box.

4 Navigate to the current unit folder	
Select **Analysis**	(If necessary) Analysis is a Word document that contains a table and graph showing the growth of sales.
Click **Insert**	

To attach the file. The Attach box appears under the Subject box and displays the name and size of the attachment.

5 Send the message	
6 Check for new messages	Click Send/Receive.
7 Observe the new message in your Inbox	

The attachment icon (a paper clip) appears to the right of the subject in the header information.

8 Open the message from your partner

9 Click **Forward**   Notice the attachment appears in the Attached field.

10 Send the message to your partner

Compressed images and image attachments

Explanation

If you are using HTML or Rich Text format for your messages, you can insert images into the message body or as attachments. If you insert or attach large pictures or several pictures, you might want to compress the pictures to make the message smaller.

Compress inserted images

After you insert pictures into a message, the Picture Tools, Format tab appears. Select the pictures you want to compress and click the Compress Pictures button. Check Apply to selected pictures only and click Options. Under Target output, select E-mail and click OK twice.

Compress image attachments

If you are sending several large images as attachments, you can resize the images before sending the message. Attach the files to the message. Then, click the Dialog Box Launcher in the Include group to display the Attachment Options task pane. Under Picture options, select Small, Medium, or Large. Complete and send your message. The recipient will receive the resized image.

Do it!

E-2: Compressing large image attachments

Here's how	Here's why
1 Open a new Message window	Click New.
2 In the To box, enter the name of your partner	To address the message to your partner.
3 In the Subject box, enter **<xx>: Spice Picture 1**	In place of <xx>, enter your partner's number.
In the message area type **Here's the first spice arrangement picture for the newsletter.**	
4 Click **Attach File**	The Attach File button is in the Include group on the Ribbon.
5 Navigate to the current unit folder	
Select **Spicearrangement1**	
Point to **Spicearrangement1**	Notice the image is 1.3 MB.
Click **Insert**	
6 Click as shown	
	To display the Attachment Options task pane.
Under Picture options, select as shown	
Click **Send**	
7 Create a new message addressed to your partner	
8 In the Subject box, enter **<xx>: Spice Picture 2**	

9 In the message area, type
**Here's the second
arrangement picture.**

Press (↵ ENTER)

10 Activate the Insert tab

Click **Picture**

Navigate to the current unit folder

Select   Notice the size of the file is approximately 1.3
Spicearrangement2.tif   MB.

Click **Insert**   To insert the picture in the body of the message.
                                        Notice the Picture Tools, Format tab appears.

11 Click **Compress Pictures**   In the Adjust group on the Picture Tools, Format
                                        tab.

Click **Options**

Under Target output, select   To optimize the picture in the message to a size
**E-mail (96 ppi): minimize   fit for e-mailing.
document size for sharing**

Click **OK**

Click **OK**

12 Click **Send**

13 Check for new messages

14 Open the Spice Picture 1 message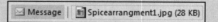

                                        Notice the attachment is a JPG file instead of a
                                        TIF file and it is considerably smaller than 1.3
                                        MB.

Close the message

15 In the Inbox Folder Contents list,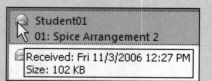
point to the Spice Picture 2
message

                                        Notice the size of the message is just over 100
                                        KB, much smaller than the original image.

Previewing and saving attachments

Explanation

When you receive a message containing a file attachment, you'll notice the message has a paperclip icon in the Folder Contents list. The icon appears to the left of the sender's name (as part of the header information). You can view the name and size of the attachment in the header of the Reading Pane or in the opened message, as shown in Exhibit 2-12.

Exhibit 2-12: An attachment

Preview or open an attachment

You can also preview the attachment in the Reading pane or the opened message by clicking the attachment. To close the attachment preview and view the message text, click Message. You can preview attachments from Office 2007 applications, such as Word, Excel, and PowerPoint. Attachment previews are supported in messages received in HTML and Plain Text format. To open an attachment, double-click the attachment.

Saving an attachment

You can either save all the attachments or save a single attachment in e-mail messages.

There are several ways to save an attachment:
- Use the File menu.
- Double-click the attachment in the Reading pane.
- Open the Message window.

To save an attachment using the File menu:
1. Display the message in the Reading pane.
2. Choose File, Save Attachments and select the name of the attached file.
3. In the Save Attachment dialog box, specify the location where you want to save the attachment.
4. Click Save.

To save an attachment by using the Reading pane, double-click the attachment. In the Opening Mail Attachment dialog box, click Save. In the Save As dialog box, specify the location where you want to save the attachment and click Save.

To save an attachment from the Message window, open the message. In the Actions group on the Ribbon, click Other Actions and choose Save Attachments, as shown in Exhibit 2-13. In the Save Attachment dialog box, specify the location where you want to save the attachment and click Save.

Exhibit 2-13: Actions group

E-3: Previewing and saving an attachment

Here's how	Here's why
1 Select the Sales Report message from your partner	To display the contents of the message in the Reading pane.
2 In the Reading pane, observe the attachment area	✉ Message ∣ 📄 Analysis.docx (20 KB) It displays a Message button and the name and size of the attachment.
3 In the Reading pane, click the attachment file name	
Click **Preview file**	To preview the attachment in the Reading pane.
Click **Message**	(In the Reading pane's attachment area.) To close the attachment preview and view the message text.
4 Double-click the attachment file name	To open the attachment in Microsoft Word. The Opening Mail Attachment dialog box might appear.
Click **Open**	(If necessary.) To open the attachment in Word.
5 Close Microsoft Word	To return to Outlook.
6 Choose **File**, **Save Attachments**, **Analysis.docx**	To open the Save Attachment dialog box.
7 Navigate to the current unit folder	
Edit the File name box to read **My sales.docx**	To save the attachment with a different name.
Click **Save**	To save the attachment and close the Save As dialog box.

Unit summary: E-mail

Topic A
In this topic, you learned that there are two main types of Outlook **e-mail accounts**: Microsoft Exchange Server and Internet e-mail accounts. You then learned that Internet e-mail accounts can use different **protocols**, such as HTTP, POP3, and IMAP4. Then, you learned how to configure a **Microsoft Exchange Server account** and two Internet accounts: an **HTTP Hotmail account**, and a **POP3 account**.

Topic B
In this topic, you learned how to work with e-mail messages. You **read a message** in the Reading pane. You also learned how to preview the first three lines of a message using **AutoPreview**.

Topic C
In this topic, you learned how to **create** and **send** a message. You learned how to use Automation features such as AutoComplete and Check Names. In addition, you used the **Ribbon** and the **Mini toolbar** to format a message. You also learned how to check the **spelling** and **grammar** in a message.

Topic D
In this topic, you replied to and resent a message by using the **Message window.** You learned that when replying to a message, you can **reply** to the sender alone or reply to all people who received the original message. Next, you learned how to **forward** a message. You then learned how to save a message as a file. You also learned how to **delete** messages and **restore** deleted messages from the Deleted Items folder.

Topic E
In this topic, you learned how to **attach** a file to a message and to **preview** and **save** an attachment. Next, you learned how to **insert and attach images** to messages and how to **compress** those **images**. Then, you learned how to preview, open, and save attachments.

Independent practice activity

In this activity, you'll attach a file to a message, check a message for spelling errors, and save an attached file. You'll also save an e-mail message as a file, and will reply to a message and forward a message.

1 Compose a message as shown in Exhibit 2-14. (*Hint:* Enter the name of your mailing partner in the To box and the message area.)

2 Attach the file New rules to the message. The New rules file is in the current unit folder.

3 Check the message for spelling errors.

4 Send the message to your partner.

5 Read the message you receive from your e-mail partner.

6 Save the attached file with the name **My new rules.txt**.

7 Save the message that you received from your mail partner as **My mail**. (*Hint*: Save it as an HTML file.)

8 Reply to the e-mail message. In the message area, enter **Thanks for the e-mail. I'll forward a copy to the purchase team.**

9 Forward the message to another student in the class other than your partner.

10 Close the Message window, if necessary.

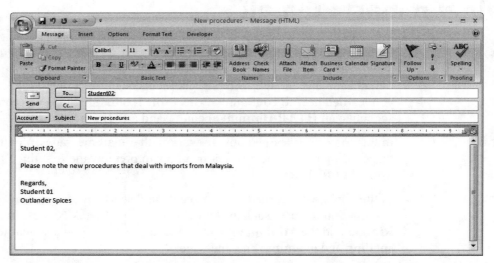

Exhibit 2-14: The Message window with a sample message for step 1 of the Independent practice activity

Review questions

1 Name some ways that you can establish a connection to the Internet.

2 What two components does a user need to access an e-mail account?

3 What is an Outlook Anywhere connection?

4 What is a protocol?

5 Which of the following are Internet e-mail protocols?

   A Microsoft Exchange Server and POP3

   B POP3 and IMAP

   C Microsoft Exchange Server and HTTP

   D NetBIOS and IMAP

6 How does Outlook connect to the Exchange Server when using an Outlook Anywhere connection?

7 When you are looking at the Folder Contents list, what is used to indicate that you've read a particular message?

8 When creating a new message, which box is used to enter the recipient's name?

9 Which feature automatically checks the address book for the recipient's name?

A AutoCorrect

B AutoComplete

C Name-checking

D Spell-checking

10 Which feature automatically enters the recipient's name based on e-mail addresses you've used earlier?

A AutoCorrect

B AutoComplete

C Name-checking

D SmartTags

11 What is the difference between using the Reply button and Reply to All button?

12 What is the procedure to attach a file to an e-mail message?

13 In what way does an e-mail's subject change when you forward a message?

14 How do you add a blind carbon copy field to a message?

15 What is AutoPreview?

16 What are the steps to quickly resend a message?

17 If you are sending several large images as attachments, how can you resize the images before sending the message?

Unit 3

E-mail management

Unit time: 50 minutes

Complete this unit, and you'll know how to:

A Set message options such as sensitivity, importance, and set up delivery and read receipt options for messages.

B Digitally sign a message, set restrictions for messages, and send an encrypted message.

C Add users to the Blocked and Safe Sender Lists, mark messages as Not Junk, empty your Junk E-mail folder, and manage junk e-mail options.

D Create and use Search folders for finding and organizing messages.

E Customize page setup options for printing, and print messages.

Topic A: Message options

This topic covers the following Microsoft Certified Application Specialist exam objectives for Outlook 2007.

#	Objective
1.4.1	**Set message sensitivity level** • Set the sensitivity of a message to confidential
1.4.2	**Set mail importance level** • Set an outgoing message to high importance • Remove a high importance flag from a message before forwarding
1.6.1	**Add or remove a flag for follow-up**
1.6.2	**Delay delivery of a message**
1.6.3	**Request read or delivery receipts**
1.6.5	**Request that replies be sent to a specific e-mail address**

Message sensitivity and importance

Explanation

When you send an e-mail message, you might want the recipient to know the sensitivity and importance of the message so that he or she can respond accordingly. You can add visual indicators to your messages to specify their importance.

Setting the sensitivity

In addition to setting the importance of a message, you can also set the *sensitivity* of a message. Sensitive e-mail messages are confidential or personal in nature. There are four levels of sensitivity: Normal (default), Personal, Private, and Confidential. When you specify the sensitivity to a setting other than Normal, a message indicating the sensitivity level will appear in the recipient's InfoBar.

To set the sensitivity of a message:

1 Create a new message.
2 Click the Dialog Box Launcher, as shown in Exhibit 3-1, in the Options group to open the Message Options dialog box, shown in Exhibit 3-2.
3 Under Message settings, select the Sensitivity level you want to use. You can also select an Importance level by using this dialog box.
4 Click Close.
5 Send the message.

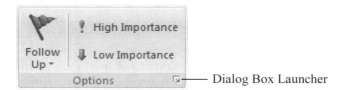

Exhibit 3-1: The Dialog Box Launcher

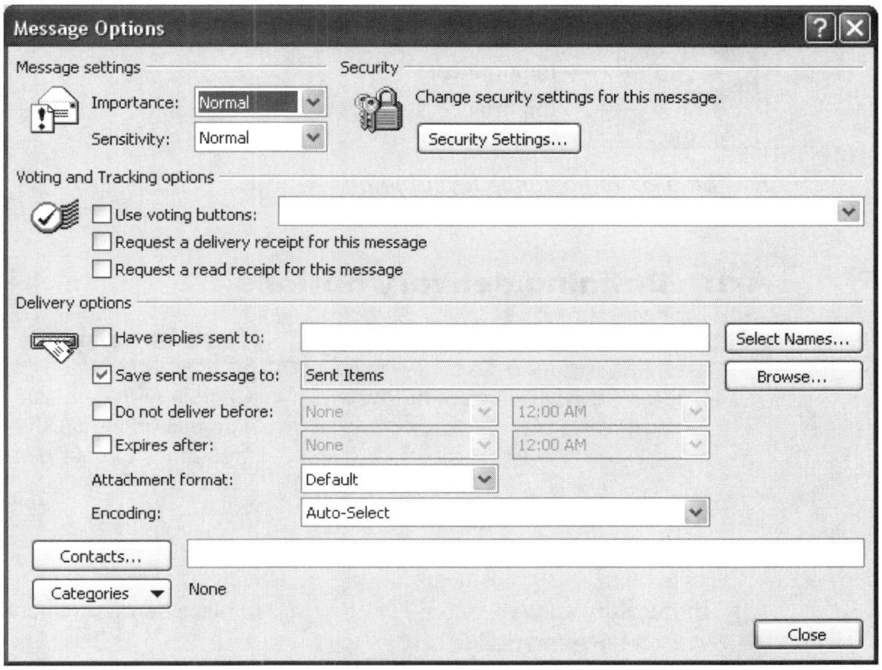

Message Options

Message settings
Importance: Normal
Sensitivity: Normal

Security
Change security settings for this message.
Security Settings...

Voting and Tracking options
☐ Use voting buttons:
☐ Request a delivery receipt for this message
☐ Request a read receipt for this message

Delivery options
☐ Have replies sent to: Select Names...
☑ Save sent message to: Sent Items   Browse...
☐ Do not deliver before: None   12:00 AM
☐ Expires after: None   12:00 AM
Attachment format: Default
Encoding: Auto-Select

Contacts...
Categories ▼   None

Close

Exhibit 3-2: The Message Options dialog box

Setting the importance

The priority of a message defines the *importance* of a message. When you set the importance level for a message to High, a red exclamation mark in the message header tells the recipient that the message needs an immediate response. The default level of importance for a message is Normal. You can also set the importance to Low for messages that don't need a response or that are not a high priority. To change importance level for a message, click either the Importance: High button or the Importance: Low button in the Options group on the Ribbon, as shown in Exhibit 3-3. If neither button is activated, then the importance level is set to Normal.

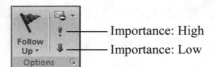 ————— Importance: High
————— Importance: Low

Exhibit 3-3: Importance level buttons

Do it!

A-1:   Defining delivery options

Here's how	Here's why
1 Open a new Message window	(Click New.) You need to know the time of a team meeting. You'll send a message of high importance to your partner.
Address the message to your partner	
In the Subject box, enter **<xx>: Personal**	In place of <xx>, enter your partner's number.
In the message area, type **Please send me the time of the team meeting.**	
2 In the Options group, click	(On the Ribbon.) To set the importance level to High.
3 Click as shown	
	(Click the Dialog Box Launcher.) To open the Message Options dialog box.
4 Under Message settings, from the Sensitivity list, select **Confidential**	
5 Click **Close**	To close the Message Options dialog box.

6 Send the message

   Click **Send/Receive**

> ✉ **Student02**   6:56 AM   ❗ ▢ ✉
> 01: Personal

To receive a message from your partner. The new message in the Folder Contents list has your student number, <yy>. The red icon to the right of the message subject indicates that the message was sent with high importance.

7 Open the message with the subject <yy>: Personal

> Please treat this as Confidential.
> This message was sent with High importance.

The InfoBar informs you that the message is confidential and was sent with high importance.

8 Click **Reply**

You'll send the time of the team meeting. Notice that the High Importance button is not selected. By default, the importance level resets to Normal when you reply to a message.

   In the message area, type
   Meeting is scheduled for 10:30 AM tomorrow.

   Send the reply

(Click Send.) The original message is still selected, and its InfoBar now indicates that you replied.

9 Click **Forward**

You'll forward this message to another person. Notice that the High Importance button is selected. The importance level does not reset to Normal when you forward a message.

10 Click **High Importance**

(In the Options group.) To remove the High importance level.

11 Send the message to another student

In the To box, enter the address of a student other than your partner. When the forwarded message is received, no exclamation point appears.

12 Close the Message window

Delay e-mail delivery

Explanation

Another e-mail message option you can specify is a delayed delivery. When you specify a delayed delivery, the message is not sent until the date and time you specify.

To specify a delayed delivery:

1 Create a new message.

2 Open the Message Options dialog box and check Do not deliver before:

- On the Message tab, in the Options group, click the Dialog Box Launcher, and in the dialog box, check Do not deliver before.

- Activate the Options tab, and in the More Options group, click Delay Delivery. "Do not deliver before" is checked automatically.

3 Next to "Do not deliver before," specify the date and time when you want the message to be sent.

4 Click Close.

5 Finish the message and click Send.

Do it!

A-2:   Specifying a delayed e-mail delivery

Here's how	Here's why
1 Open a new Message window	
Address the message to your partner	
In the Subject box, enter **<xx>: Reminder**	In place of <xx>, enter your partner's number.
2 In the message area, type **Don't forget we have a meeting at 10:30.**	The meeting you're referencing is scheduled for tomorrow, so you'll delay the message to be sent tomorrow.
3 Activate the Options tab	
4 Click **Delay Delivery**	(In the More Options group.) To open the Message Options dialog box. Under Delivery options, "Do not deliver before" is checked.
5 From the list next to Do not deliver before, select tomorrow's date	
6 From the time list, select **8:00 AM**	To specify the time at which the e-mail message can be sent.
7 Click **Close**	
8 Click **Send**	To send the message. It won't be received until after 8 AM tomorrow.

Specify e-mail reply addresses

Explanation

By default, when a recipient replies to an e-mail message, the reply is sent back to the original sender's address. However, when you send a message, you might want replies to be sent to a different address. For example, if you use more than one e-mail account, you might send a message from one account, but you want replies to go to another of your e-mail accounts. Alternately, you might want a response to go to a colleague.

To specify an e-mail address to which replies are sent:

1 Create a new message.

2 Open the Message Options dialog box and check Have replies sent to:

- On the Message tab, in the Options group, click the Dialog Box Launcher, and in the dialog box, check Have replies sent to.

- Activate the Options tab, and in the More Options group click Direct Replies To. "Have replies sent to" is checked automatically.

3 Next to "Have replies sent to," specify the e-mail address to which you want replies sent.

4 Click Close.

5 Finish the message and click Send.

Do it!

A-3: Specifying an e-mail reply address

Here's how	Here's why
1 Open a new Message window	
Address the message to your partner	
In the Subject box, enter **<xx>: Out Thursday**	In place of <xx>, enter your partner's number.
2 In the message area, type **I'll be out of town Thursday. Contact me in an emergency.**	You'll specify your personal e-mail address for any replies to this message, because while you're out of town, you'll be checking your personal e-mail.
3 Activate the Options tab	
4 Click **Direct Replies To**	(In the More Options group.) To open the Message Options dialog box. Under Delivery options, "Have replies sent to" is checked.
5 Next to Have replies sent to, enter an alternate e-mail address	Specify an alternate e-mail address provided by your instructor. If no alternate is available, just specify your assigned e-mail address.
6 Click **Close**	
7 Click **Send**	

Message flags

Explanation   When you receive an e-mail message that you need to follow up on, you can identify the message by flagging it. You can also send a flagged message to other people. The message will then alert the recipient that immediate action is needed for that message. Flagged messages create to-do items either for you alone or for you and the recipients of the e-mail message.

If your Inbox contains many e-mail messages, you might think it will be difficult to search for flagged messages. Flagged messages are displayed in the Task list on the To-Do bar, as shown in Exhibit 3-4.

Exhibit 3-4: Flagged messages in the To-Do bar's Task list

Flagging received messages

Flagging a message identifies it for further action by inserting a flag symbol to the right of the message in the Folder Contents list. When you flag a received message, you can specify the action to be taken, the due date, and the time. To flag a message, right-click the flag column to the right of the message and select one of the menu options as shown in Exhibit 3-5. After you set the flag, the InfoBar displays the option that you chose. Your flagged message will appear in the To-Do bar, in Tasks, and in the Daily Task list in Calendar.

Exhibit 3-5: Flag menu

Mark a flagged message as completed

After you follow up on a flagged message, you can mark the flag as completed. You can work with flagged messages in either the To-Do bar's Task list or in the Folder Contents list. To mark a flag as complete, either click the message's flag column or right-click the message and choose Follow Up, Mark Complete. When marked as completed, the flag changes to a check mark and the message is removed from the To-Do bar's Task list.

Clear a message flag

If you want to remove the flag from an e-mail message, use the Clear Flag option. When you clear a flag, there is no record of the message ever appearing in views such as the To-Do bar and Tasks. If you want to keep a record of completed items, use the Mark Complete option.

A-4: Flagging an e-mail message

Here's how	Here's why
1 Open the Inbox	If necessary.
2 Open a new Message window	
Address the message to your partner	You'll send a message to a client (your partner) so that he or she can set up an appointment.
Specify the subject as **<xx>: Marketing meeting**	In place of <xx>, enter your partner's number.
In the message area, type **There will be an informal marketing meeting today at 1 PM.**	
3 Send the message	
4 Create a new message addressed to your partner	
Specify the subject as **<xx>: Sales meeting**	
In the message area, type **There will be a sales meeting tomorrow at 2 PM.**	
5 Send the message	
6 Check for new messages	
	To receive two messages from your partner. The new messages appear in the Folder Contents list with colorless flag icons to the right.
7 Select the Marketing meeting message	
Click the flag icon	
	To flag the message for follow-up. Notice that the message now has a red flag and appears in your To-Do bar under Today. By default, flagged messages are flagged under Today.

8 Select the Sales meeting message

Right-click the flag icon

Choose **Tomorrow**

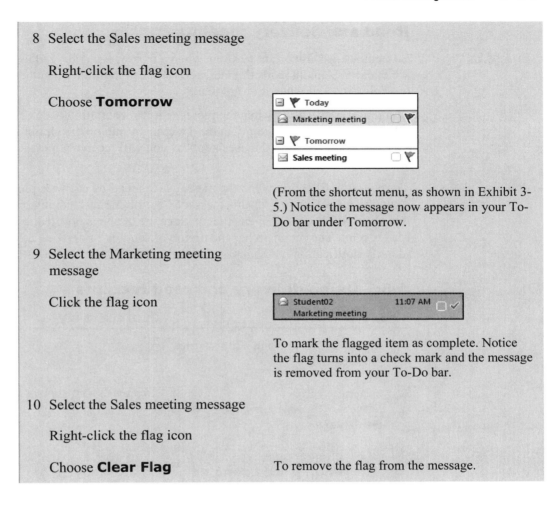

(From the shortcut menu, as shown in Exhibit 3-5.) Notice the message now appears in your To-Do bar under Tomorrow.

9 Select the Marketing meeting message

Click the flag icon

To mark the flagged item as complete. Notice the flag turns into a check mark and the message is removed from your To-Do bar.

10 Select the Sales meeting message

Right-click the flag icon

Choose **Clear Flag**

To remove the flag from the message.

Read and delivery receipts

Explanation

Sometimes, it's important to know when a message is delivered to the recipient and when each recipient reads the message. You can monitor when the messages you sent are delivered and when they are read.

To request notification when the message has successfully been delivered, check "Request a Delivery Receipt" in the Tracking group on the Options tab. When the message is delivered to the user's Inbox, you will receive a message stating that delivery was successful.

To request notification when the message was read by each recipient, check the "Request a read receipt for this message" option in the Tracking group on the Options tab. When the recipient opens the message, he or she is notified that you've requested a read receipt. The recipient has the option of sending or denying a read receipt. You can identify notification messages in your Inbox by the word "Read:" before the subject.

Do it!

A-5:   Using delivery and read receipts

Here's how	Here's why
1 Create a message and address it to your partner	
Enter the subject **<xx>: Cinnamon prices in Malaysia**	In place of <xx>, enter your partner's number.
In the message area, type **Cinnamon prices doubled today. We'll need to revise our prices.**	
2 Activate the Options tab	
In the Tracking group, check **Request a Delivery Receipt**	You'll receive a return message with the date and time the message was delivered to the recipient's Inbox.
In the Tracking group, check **Request a Read Receipt**	You'll receive a return message with the date and time when the recipient opens the message.
3 Send the message to your partner	
4 Check for new messages	To receive a message from your partner.
5 Open the message with the subject <yy>: Cinnamon Prices in Malaysia	A message box appears, prompting you to send a read receipt to the sender.
Check **Don't ask me about sending receipts again**	To specify that you don't want to display this message box again.
Click **Yes**	To send the read receipt message.
6 Close the Message window	

7 Check for new messages	There will be two new messages in the Folder Contents list. One is the delivery receipt and the other is a read receipt for the message you sent to your partner.
8 Select the delivery-receipt message	(From the Folder Contents list.) The Reading pane displays the information about delivering the e-mail message.
9 Select the read-receipt message	**Student01** Read: 02: Cinnamon prices in Malaysia "Read:" precedes the subject of this message. The Reading pane displays the details about the e-mail message and when it was read.

Topic B: E-mail security

This topic covers the following Microsoft Certified Application Specialist exam objectives for Outlook 2007.

#	Objective
1.5.1	Digitally sign a message
1.5.2	Restrict permissions to a message
1.5.3	Encrypt a message

Restricting permissions to messages

Explanation

Information Rights Management (IRM) allows individuals to specify access permissions to e-mail messages. To use IRM in Outlook 2007, your computer must have the Windows Rights Management Services (RMS) Client Service Pack 1 (SP1) or higher installed on your computer. Most likely this software will be installed on your computer by an RMS or Exchange administrator.

Depending on the configuration of RMS in your organization, you might be able to use IRM to:

- Prevent restricted content from being forwarded, copied, modified, printed, or faxed.
- Prevent restricted content from being copied by using the Print Screen feature in Microsoft Windows.
- Restrict content wherever it is sent.
- Provide the same level of restriction to e-mail attachments that were created by using other Microsoft Office programs, such as Microsoft Office Word 2007, Microsoft Office Excel 2007, or Microsoft Office PowerPoint 2007.
- Set an expiration date for the restricted content so that it can no longer be viewed after a specified period of time.

Sending restricted messages

To send an e-mail message with restricted permission:

1 Create a new message.

2 Click the Office button and click Permission.

3 To use your company's custom permission policy, click the arrow next to Permission and select the permission policy.

 The message's InfoBar will display Do Not Forward, indicating that the message is restricted. The message recipients will not be able to forward, print, or copy the message content.

4 Send the message.

Opening restricted messages

If your computer does not have the Windows RMS Client installed and you try to open a restricted message, Outlook 2007 will prompt you to download the software. Check with your administrator before downloading and installing the RMS Client on your computer.

If you need to read or open content with restricted content and your organization does not use RMS, you can download the Rights Management Add-on for Internet Explorer. With this add-on, you can only view restricted messages. You will not be able to reply to, forward, copy, or print the messages. In addition, you cannot view any attachments when using the Internet Explorer Rights Management Add-on.

The first time that you attempt to open a message with restricted permission, you must connect to a licensing server to verify your credentials and to download a use license. The use license defines the level of access that you have to a file.

Messages with restricted permission that you receive can be identified by the icon that appears next to the message in the message list of your Inbox. You cannot view the contents of a rights-managed message in the Reading pane. You must open the message to view its contents.

B-1: Discussing restricted messages

Questions and answers

1 What is IRM?

2 What types of restrictions can you place on a message using IRM?

3 If you need to read or open content with restricted content and your organization does not use RMS, what can you do?

4 What happens the first time that you attempt to open a message with restricted permission?

5 What is a use license?

Digitally signing messages

Explanation

You can send digitally signed messages to prove your identity and prevent message tampering. To send digitally signed messages, you must first obtain a digital ID from a certifying authority (CA).

To obtain a digital ID:

1 Choose Tools, Trust Center.
2 On the left side of the Trust Center dialog box, click E-mail Security.
3 Under Digital IDs (Certificates), click Get a Digital ID.
4 Outlook starts your Web browser and opens a Web page on the Microsoft Office Marketplace Web site that lists several certification authorities.
5 Click the one that you want to use and follow the instructions on the Web page to register for a digital ID. The cost for a digital ID varies. Digital IDs are available for commercial use or personal use. The certification authority will then send you a digital ID and instructions via e-mail.

Note: Your company might provide a digital ID in your setup. Ask your administrator if you need to obtain a digital ID.

Sending a digitally signed message

By digitally signing a message, you apply your signature to the message. The digital signature includes your certificate and public key. This information proves to the recipient that you signed the contents of the message, and not an imposter, and that the contents have not been altered in transit.

You can digitally sign on a per-message basis or you can specify that all messages be digitally signed. To sign on a per-message basis, click the Digitally Sign Message button in the Options group on the Message tab. You then compose your message and send it. However, the first time you digitally sign an individual message, the Digitally Sign Message button might not appear. In that case, you need to perform the following steps to digitally sign the message:

1 Open a message window.
2 In the Options group, click the Dialog Box Launcher to open the Message Options dialog box.
3 Click Security Settings to open the Security Properties dialog box.
4 Check Add digital signature to this message.
5 Click OK.
6 Click Close. When you open new message windows from this point on, the Digitally Sign Message button will appear, as shown in Exhibit 3-6, and you can simply click it to add a digital signature.

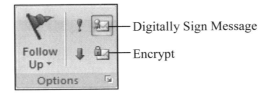

Exhibit 3-6: The Digitally Sign Message button in the Options group

Another way to digitally sign messages is by specifying that all messages be signed. To digitally sign all messages:

1 Choose Tools, Trust Center.

2 On the left, click E-mail Security.

3 Under Encrypted e-mail, check Add digital signature to outgoing messages.

4 If you want recipients who don't have S/MIME security to be able to read the message, verify that the "Send clear text signed message when sending signed messages" options is checked.

5 Click OK.

Do it!

B-2: Digitally signing a message

Here's how	Here's why
1 Choose **Tools**, **Trust Center...**	To open the Trust Center dialog box. You'll apply for a digital ID.
Select **E-mail Security**	In the left column.
2 Click **Get a Digital ID**	(Under Digital IDs (Certificates).) Your default Web browser will open and display the Microsoft Office Marketplace Web site.
Click **Yes**	If necessary, click Yes to open or add the site to your Trusted sites list. You might need to click Yes several times.
3 Click **Comodo Web site**	Under Available digital IDs. Comodo currently offers free digital IDs for personal use.
4 Click **GET YOUR FREE EMAIL CERT NOW**	
5 Fill out the form and agree to the terms	When you've successfully completed the forms, a message with your digital ID information will be sent to your e-mail address.
6 Check for new messages	
Follow the instructions to install the certificate	
7 Create a new mail message with the subject **Digitally signed**	
Address the message to your partner's POP3 e-mail account	You'll add a digital signature to the message.
8 In the Options group, click the Dialog Box Launcher	To open the Message Options dialog box.

9	Click **Security Settings**	To open the Security Properties dialog box.
	Check **Add digital signature to this message**	
	Click **OK**	To return to the Message Options dialog box.
10	Click **Close**	In the future, when you create new messages, the Digitally Sign Message button will appear automatically in the Options group, as shown in Exhibit 3-6, and you can simply click it to add a digital signature.
11	Click the Account button, and select the account the certificate is signed for	If necessary.
	Send your message	
12	Check for new messages	

> Student02   10:40 AM
> Digitally signed

Notice the new message from your partner indicates that it is digitally signed.

13	Open the message	You'll view the digital signature.
	Click	To the right of the Signed by line in the message header.
	Click **Details**	To view the information about the digital signature.
	Click **Close** twice	
14	Close the message window	

Encrypting messages

Explanation

Cryptography is a set of standards and protocols for encoding data and messages, so that they can be stored and transmitted more securely. The two fundamental operations of cryptography are encryption and decryption. Encryption scrambles the data so it is impossible to figure out the original information. When the message is decrypted, the scrambled data is turned back into the original text by using a decryption key.

Outlook uses certificates in cryptographic e-mail messaging to help provide more secure communications. To use cryptography when you send and receive e-mail messages, you must first obtain a digital ID from a certificate authority (CA).

Similar to sending digitally signed messages, you can either encrypt a single message or encrypt all outgoing messages. To encrypt a single message, create a new message. Then click the Encrypt Message Contents and Attachments button in the Options group on the Message tab. Compose and send your message.

To encrypt all outgoing messages:

1 Choose Tools, Trust Center.

2 On the left, click E-mail Security.

3 Under Encrypted e-mail, check Encrypt contents and attachments for outgoing messages.

4 Click OK.

To send encrypted messages over the Internet, you need to exchange certificates (CER files) with the recipient. There are several ways to exchange certificates:

- Send the recipient a digitally signed message. The recipient adds your e-mail name to Contacts and in doing so, also adds your certificate.

- Send an e-mail message with your CER file attached. The recipient can import the CER file into your contact card.

- Create a contact card with your CER file and send the contact card to the recipient.

Do it!

B-3: Sending an encrypted message

Here's how	Here's why
1 Select the digitally signed message from your e-mail partner	
Right-click your partner's e-mail address	In the Reading Pane.
Choose **Add to Outlook Contacts**	A Contact window opens displaying your partner's contact information.
Click **Save & Close**	Your partner's certificate is automatically stored with the contact file, and can be used with any e-mails to that address.

2 Create a new message with the subject **Encrypted message**	You'll send an encrypted message to your partner.
Address the message to your partner's POP3 account	
Enter a short message	
3 In the Options group, click [icon]	To encrypt the message.
4 Send the message from your digitally signed account	Use the Account button to select it if necessary.
5 Check for new messages	

Notice the new message from your partner indicates that it is encrypted.

6 Select the message	This encrypted e-mail cannot be displayed in the Reading Pane.
Open the message to read it.

Notice that the Reading pane tells you the message is encrypted and you must open the message to read it.

7 Open the message

Click [icon]

To open the Message Security Properties dialog box, in which you can read information about the encryption.

8 Close the dialog box and the message

Topic C: Junk e-mail

This topic covers the following Microsoft Certified Application Specialist exam objective for Outlook 2007.

#	Objective
5.3.5	**Manage Junk e-mail messages** • Add users to the Blocked Senders List • Add users or domains to the Safe Senders List • Empty the Junk e-mail message folder • Mark a message as Not Junk

Blocked Senders Lists

Explanation

You might get a number of unwanted or junk e-mail messages, which can clog your Inbox if not managed properly. *Junk e-mail messages* include messages such as business promotion messages, advertisements, or messages with adult content. Outlook provides a folder called Junk E-mail to store such messages.

Blocked Senders List

You can block messages from a sender by adding the sender's e-mail address or domain name to the Blocked Senders List. When you add a name or e-mail address to this list, Outlook places incoming message from that sender in the Junk E-mail folder.

There are two ways to add a sender to the Blocked Senders list:

- In the Folder Contents list, right-click the message and choose Junk E-mail, Add Sender to Blocked Senders List.

- Choose Tools, Options to open the Options dialog box. Under E-mail, click Junk E-mail. Activate the Blocked Senders tab. Click Add. Enter the e-mail address or domain name for the sender you want to block and click OK. Click OK twice to close the dialog boxes and save your changes.

Do it!   **C-1:   Adding senders to the Blocked Senders Lists**

Here's how	Here's why
1 Activate Contacts	First, you'll make sure your partner is not listed in your Contacts because all e-mail addresses in your Contacts are by default included in the Safe Senders List.
Right-click the contact for your partner	If necessary.
Choose **Delete**	
2 Right-click the Digitally signed message from your partner	
Choose **Junk E-mail, Add Sender to Blocked Senders List**	
Click **OK**	To clear the message stating the message was moved to your Junk E-mail folder.
3 Create a new message with the subject **Blocked message**	Make sure your partner completes step 1 before performing this step.
Address and send it to your partner	Use POP3 addresses for both you and your partner.
4 Check for new messages	A message might appear, indicating that a message has been moved to the Junk E-mail folder.
Click **Close**	If necessary.
5 Select the Junk E-mail folder	The new message from your partner is sent directly to the Junk E-mail folder.

The Junk E-mail folder

Explanation

Any message that is caught by the Junk E-mail filter is moved to a special Junk E-mail folder. It is a good idea to review the messages in the Junk E-mail folder from time to time to make sure that they are not legitimate messages that you want to see. If they are legitimate, you can move them back to the Inbox by marking them as not junk. You can also drag them to any folder. After you review the messages in your Junk E-mail folder, you can then empty the folder.

Marking a message as not junk

Depending on the Junk E-mail filter's protection level, some messages that you want to see might be moved to the Junk E-mail folder instead. For this reason, it is recommended that you periodically review the messages in your Junk E-mail folder to ensure that you are not missing any legitimate messages.

To mark a particular message as not junk, follow these steps:

1 In Mail, select the Junk E-mail folder.
2 Right-click any message that you want to mark as not junk and choose Junk E-mail, Mark as Not Junk.
3 Notice you have the option to always trust e-mail from this recipient. Uncheck the box if you don't want to always trust e-mail from the recipient. Click OK.

The message that is marked as not junk is moved either to your Inbox or to the folder in which it was previously located.

Emptying the Junk E-mail folder

To empty the Junk E-mail folder, right-click the Junk E-mail folder and choose Empty "Junk E-mail" Folder. Emptying and deleting messages from the Junk E-mail folder only moves the messages to the Deleted Items folder. To delete messages permanently, empty the Deleted Items folder as well.

Do it!

C-2:   Marking a message as not junk

Here's how	Here's why
1 Right-click the Blocked message from your partner	In the Junk E-mail folder.
Choose **Junk E-mail, Mark as Not Junk...**	
Click **OK**	Notice the default option is to always trust e-mail from this recipient.
2 Right-click the Junk E-mail folder	
Choose **Empty "Junk E-mail" Folder**	
Click **Yes**	

Safe Senders list

Explanation

By default, all of the e-mail addresses in your Contacts are included in the Safe Senders list. E-mail addresses and domain names in the Safe Senders list are never treated as junk e-mail, regardless of the content of the message.

You can also add senders to your Safe Senders list by doing one of the following:

- In the Folder Contents list, right-click the message and choose Junk E-mail, Add Sender to Safe Senders List.
- Choose Tools, Options to open the Options dialog box. Under E-mail, click Junk E-mail. Activate the Safe Senders tab. Click Add. Enter the e-mail address or domain for the sender you want to allow and click OK. Click OK twice to close the dialog boxes and save your changes.

Do it!

C-3: Adding senders to the Safe Senders list

Here's how	Here's why
1 View your Inbox	You'll add your partner to your Safe Sender List.
2 Right-click a message from your partner Choose **Junk E-mail, Add Sender to Safe Senders List** Click **OK**	
3 Choose **Actions, Junk E-mail, Junk E-mail Options...**	To open the Junk E-mail Options dialog box. You'll also add a domain to your Safe Sender list.
4 Activate the Safe Senders tab	On this tab, you can store the e-mail addresses of the people you trust to send valid messages. Messages from these e-mail addresses are sent directly to your Inbox.
5 Click **Add**	To open the Add address or domain dialog box. You can specify the e-mail addresses of trusted senders in this dialog box.
6 Enter **@outlanderspices.com**	(Type @outlanderspices.com and press Enter.) To allow messages from any sender that has an outlanderspices.com e-mail address.
7 Check **Automatically add people I e-mail to the Safe Senders List**	This setting will add everyone you e-mail to the Safe Senders list. One drawback to this setting is that if you send a message to remove yourself from a spam list, then that address will end up on your Safe Senders list.
8 Click **OK**	

Junk e-mail options

Explanation

The Junk E-mail Options dialog box provides four options for filtering junk e-mail, as shown in Exhibit 3-7. By default, Low is selected and the most obvious junk e-mail messages are sent to your Junk E-mail folder. Any message that satisfies the conditions specified in this dialog box is moved to the Junk E-mail folder. You can also check an option to permanently delete suspected junk e-mail instead of moving it to the Junk E-Mail folder. However, legitimate messages might be deleted using this option.

To set the options for filtering junk e-mail:

1 Choose Actions, Junk E-mail, Junk Email Options to open the Junk E-mail Options dialog box, shown in Exhibit 3-7.

2 Set the relevant options to filter the incoming messages.

3 Click OK to close the Junk E-mail Options dialog box.

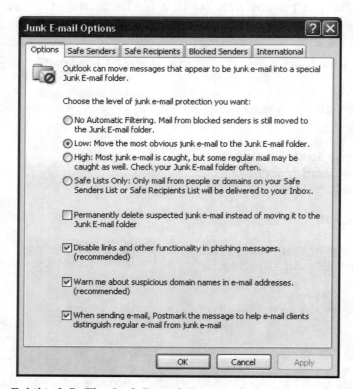

Exhibit 3-7: The Junk E-mail Options dialog box

Phishing messages

In Outlook 2007, the Junk-E-mail filter can evaluate your incoming messages to see whether they are phishing messages. Phishing messages try to trick you into entering your personal information, such as your bank account number or a password. Phishing messages often contain suspicious links and are sent from a spoofed (fake) e-mail address. If the filter determines that a message is suspicious, the message is sent to the Junk E-mail folder, the message format is changed to plain text format, and the links are disabled.

Outlook e-mail postmarking

Another way to manage junk e-mail is through *postmarking*. When this feature is enabled, as shown in Exhibit 3-7, Outlook stamps each message with a digital postmark that incorporates the unique characteristics of the message. Each postmark is valid for a single message and it takes a little more time to construct the postmark. As a result, it takes a little longer to send a message. For the average e-mail user, this time is insignificant. For spammers, this feature would slow them down so it's likely they won't use this feature. Incoming messages that aren't postmarked are marked as spam and sent to your Junk E-mail folder.

Do it!

C-4: Changing junk e-mail options

Here's how	Here's why
1 Choose **Actions, Junk E-mail, Junk E-mail Options...**	To open the Junk E-mail Options dialog box. Notice that the protection level is set to low. You can also use the other options to set the protection level for messages. Also notice that the filter is set to disable links in phishing messages, warn you about suspicious domain names, and postmark outgoing messages.
2 Select **High**	To change the level of protection so that more junk e-mail is caught and sent to your Junk E-mail folder.
3 Activate the Blocked Senders tab	You can use this tab to store the e-mail addresses of those who send junk messages.
Click **Add**	To open the Add address or domain dialog box. You can specify junk e-mail addresses in this dialog box.
Click **Cancel**	
4 Activate the International tab	You can use this tab to block addresses from other countries or to block messages written in foreign languages.
5 Click **OK**	To close the Junk E-mail Options dialog box.

Topic D: Search folders

This topic covers the following Microsoft Certified Application Specialist exam objective for Outlook 2007.

#	Objective
5.4.5	Create a custom Search folder

Creating Search folders

Explanation

In Outlook, you can create your own *Search folders* for storing messages in a specific category or based on a specific condition. For example, if you create a Search folder to store all the messages containing specific text, all such messages are stored in the Search folder.

To create a Search folder:

1 In the Navigation Pane, click Mail.
2 In the Mail pane, right-click Search folders.
3 Choose New Search Folder to open the New Search Folder dialog box, shown in Exhibit 3-8.
4 From the Select a Search Folder list, select a condition.
5 Click OK.

Exhibit 3-8: The New Search Folder dialog box

Do it!   **D-1:   Setting up a Search folder**

Here's how	Here's why
1 Activate the Mail pane	If necessary.
2 Right-click **Search Folders**	(Search Folders appears in the Mail pane.) A shortcut menu appears.
Choose **New Search Folder...**	To open the New Search Folder dialog box.
3 Under Organizing Mail, select **Mail with specific words**	To specify the condition.
Click **Choose**	To open the Search Text dialog box.
4 In the box, enter as shown	Specify words or phrases to search for in the subject or body: Welcome
Click **Add**	The word "Welcome" is added to the Search list.
Click **OK**	To close the Search Text dialog box.
5 Click **OK**	To close the New Search Folder dialog box.
6 Observe the Mail pane and the Folder Contents list	In the Mail pane, the Search Folders folder is expanded. All messages with the text "Welcome" in their subject or body appear in the Folder Contents list.

Click as shown	Search Folders
	   Categorized Mail
	   Containing Welcome
	   Large Mail
	   Unread Mail

	To collapse the Search Folders folder.

Using Search folders

Explanation

After creating a Search folder, you can use it to store mail messages that satisfy the Search folder's condition. For example, you can create a Search folder to store all messages to or from a specific client.

To see the mail messages in a Search folder, expand Search folders and click the name of the Search folder you want to use. The Search folder's contents appear in the Folder Contents list.

Do it!

D-2: Using a Search folder

Here's how	Here's why
1 Open the Inbox folder	Activate the Mail pane, and then click Inbox.
2 Open a new Message window	Click the New button.
3 Address the message to your partner	In the To box, enter the name of your partner.
In the Subject box, enter **<xx>: Welcome to the meeting**	In place of <xx>, enter your partner's number.
Type any text of your choice in the message area	
4 Send the message	
5 Check for new messages	To receive your partner's message.
6 Expand Search folders	Click the plus sign near Search folders. Notice that the Containing Welcome (1) folder name appears in bold in the Mail pane.
7 Click **Containing Welcome (1)**	(This link is in the Mail pane.) To view the contents of the specific folder. The new message with the word "Welcome" in the subject appears in the Folder Contents list, along with all other messages containing the word "Welcome."
8 Open the message with the subject <yy>: Welcome to the meeting	To read the contents of the message.
Close the Message window	

Topic E: Printing messages

Explanation

As with other Office documents, you can print Outlook messages. You can also control page settings such as margins, headers and footers, and orientation.

Page setup

You can customize the way messages print by configuring the page setup. By default, a message prints in the Memo style. To customize the page setup for all messages that use the Memo style, choose File, Page Setup, Memo Style. You can create new print styles by choosing File, Page Setup, Define Print Styles.

The Page Setup: Memo Style dialog box is shown in Exhibit 3-9. You can use the Format, Paper, and Header/Footer tabs to specify the fonts, paper source, margins, orientation, and the header and footer that should appear in the printed message. A header will appear at the top of the page, and the footer will appear at the bottom of the page. A page layout preview appears on the Format tab.

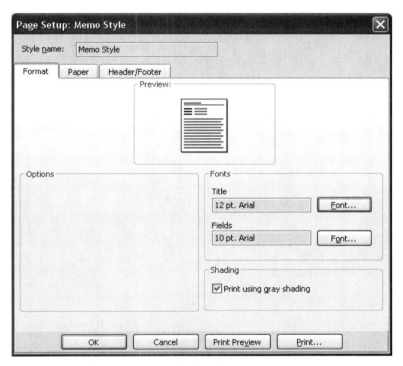

Exhibit 3-9: The Page Setup dialog box

Do it!   **E-1:   Customizing page setup for printing**

Here's how	Here's why
1 Choose **File**, **Page Setup**, **Memo Style**	To open the Page Setup: Memo Style dialog box. You'll add a header that will appear for all e-mail messages that use the Memo style.
2 Activate the Header/Footer tab	
3 In the first Header box, enter **Outlander Spices**	
Click **OK**	To close the Page Setup dialog box.

Printing messages

Explanation

You can print a message from both the Folder Contents list and the Message window. To send the message selected in the Folder Contents list to the printer without opening the Print dialog box, click the Print button on the Standard toolbar. Use the File, Print command from the Folder Contents list when you want to change the print style.

To open the Print dialog box from a Message window, click the Office button and choose Print.

The Print dialog box displays the selected printing style. To change the print style settings, click the Page Setup button. In the Print dialog box, you can specify details such as the printer you want to use, the number of pages, number of copies, and whether attached files should print.

To print a message:

1 Open a message in the Message window.

2 Click the Office button and click Print to open the Print dialog box, shown in Exhibit 3-10.

3 Under Copies, from the Number of pages list, select the number of pages you want to print. By default, All is selected.

4 In the Number of copies box, specify the number of copies you want to print.

5 To change the printing style settings, such as paper size and orientation, click the Page Setup button.

6 Click OK to print the document.

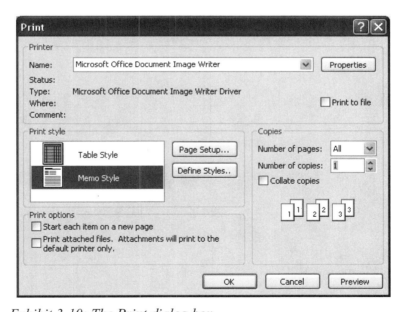

Exhibit 3-10: The Print dialog box

Do it!

E-2: Printing a message

Here's how	Here's why
1 Open the message with the subject \<yy\>: Venue for the class	Where \<yy\> is your student number.
2 Click	(In the upper-left corner of the program window.) To display a menu of commonly used file commands.
Choose **Print**	To open the Print dialog box.
3 Observe the dialog box	The name of the printer appears in the Name box. Under Copies, All is selected for the number of pages and by default, one copy will be printed.
4 Click **Cancel**	To close the Print dialog box without printing the message.
5 Close the Message window	

Unit summary:E-mail management

Topic A   In this topic, you learned how to **set importance** and **sensitivity levels** for messages. You also specified **delayed delivery** for an e-mail, and specified an alternate address for e-mail replies. Then, you learned how to **flag messages** and **mark** flagged messages as **completed.** You also learned how to request a **read receipt**.

Topic B   In this topic, you learned how to use e-mail security features such as **Information Rights Management (IRM)**, digital signatures, and encryption. You learned that IRM requires having the **Rights Management Services (RMS) Client** installed on your computer. You also learned that you can use IRM to prevent **restricted content** from being forwarded, copied, modified, printed, or faxed. You then learned how to obtain a **digital ID** and how to use it to create **digitally signed** and **encrypted** messages.

Topic C   In this topic, you learned how to manage **junk e-mail**. You learned to add senders to the **Blocked Senders list**. You also learned how to add senders and domains to the **Safe Senders List**. Then you learned how to mark a message as **not junk** and to empty the **Junk E-mail folder**. You also learned how to change the **junk e-mail level** and how to automatically add recipients to your Safe Senders list.

Topic D   In this topic, you learned how to **create** and **use Search folders,** which are used to search for and store messages that meet a certain condition.

Topic E   In this topic, you learned how to customize **page setup** for printing messages; page setup options include paper, headers and footers, margins, and orientation. You also learned how to **print** a message by using the **Print dialog box**.

Independent practice activity

In this activity, you'll specify a read receipt and an importance level for a new message. You'll create a flagged message, reply to a flagged message, send an encrypted and digitally signed message, and change your junk e-mail settings. You'll also add a sender to your Safe Senders list and modify the page setup for the Memo Style.

1   Compose a message with the text, **I forgot the date for the project-planning meeting. Can you please remind me?** Address the message to your partner.

2   Specify the subject as **Forgot**.

3   Set the options so that you receive a read receipt.

4   Set the importance level to High.

5   Send the message.

6   Open the read receipt and read it. (*Hint*: Activate the Inbox.)

7   Close the Message window.

8   Create a flagged message to reply by 4:30 PM today, and send it to your partner. Specify any subject and message text. (*Hint*: In the Options group on the Message tab, click **Follow Up** and choose **Flag for Recipients**.)

9   Reply to the flagged message and mark the flagged message as completed.

10   Send an encrypted, digitally signed message to your partner.

11   Change the junk e-mail level to Low. (*Hint*: Choose **Actions**, **Junk E-mail**, **Junk E-mail Options**.)

12   Turn off the setting that automatically adds recipients to your Safe Senders list.

13 Add samwilkens@doverspiceworks.com to your Safe Senders list.

14 Remove the header from the Memo style and add **Outlander Spices** as a footer to appear on the left side of the document. (*Hint*: Choose **File**, **Page Setup**, **Memo Style**.)

Review questions

1 On the Message tab, which group contains the buttons for setting the importance of a message?

A Send

B Options

C Names

D Editing

2 What is the advantage of marking a message as private?

3 What does a red exclamation mark indicate?

4 What can you use to prevent restricted content from being forwarded, copied, modified, printed, or faxed?

5 If your company doesn't allow installing the RMS Client, how can you still read a restricted message?

6 Which of the following messages cannot be viewed in the Reading pane? (Choose all that apply.)

A High Importance flagged message

B High Sensitivity flagged message

C Encrypted message

D Restricted message

D Digitally signed message

7 To send digitally signed or encrypted messages, what must you first obtain?

8 What does a digital signature include?

9 How can you block messages from an entire domain?

10 True or false? You should just delete all messages in your Junk E-mail folder without reviewing them.

11 What should you do if a legitimate e-mail message ends up in your Junk E-mail folder?

12 When using a Search folder, when do you specify the condition that controls which messages are stored in the folder?

A After naming the new folder

B After adding the folder to the Folder Contents list

C While creating the new folder

D After saving the new folder

13 What is the purpose of Search folders?

14 Name two ways to flag a message.

15 When sending an urgent message, what can you do to be alerted when the recipient reads your message?

16 What is the difference between clicking the Print button on the Standard toolbar and choosing File, Print in the Folder Contents list (or clicking the Office button and choosing Print in an open message) to print a message?

Unit 4

Contact management

Unit time: 60 minutes

Complete this unit, and you'll know how to:

A Use the Contacts folder to add new business and personal contacts, modify existing contacts, and organize contacts.

B Create and modify a distribution list.

C Create and send an electronic business card to message recipients; add formatting to your electronic business card; and create a contact from an electronic business card.

Topic A: Managing contacts

This topic covers the following Microsoft Certified Application Specialist exam objectives for Outlook 2007.

#	Objective
4.1.1	**Create a contact from a blank contact**
	• Create a new contact
	• Create a new contact based on another contact
4.1.2	**Create a contact from a message header**
4.1.4	**Save a contact received as a contact record**
4.1.5	**Modify contact information**
	• Modify a contact and save it to update the existing contact
	• Modify a contact and save it as a new contact
	• Add a document, message, or other information to a contact

The Contact window

Explanation

A *contact* is a person with whom you have either a business or a personal relationship. You use the Contacts folder to manage information about each contact, such as the person's name, address, telephone number, e-mail address, Web page address, company name, birthday, and anniversary. The Contacts folder is integrated with the Inbox and the Calendar for sending e-mail and scheduling meetings. For example, when you enter a contact's birthday, it's automatically entered in the Calendar.

You can view the Contacts pane and folder by clicking Contacts in the Navigation pane. You add or edit contacts by using the Contact window. To add a new contact, click New on the Standard toolbar. Enter the contact's information and click Save & Close. To edit a contact, double-click the contact in the Folder Content list.

The Ribbon in the Contact window has the following three tabs:

- **Contact:** Contains controls to show contact information, contact a contact, save a contact, and share a contact. You can use the buttons in the Show group to access pages that contain specific contact information. These buttons are General, Details, Activities, Certificates, and All Fields. The General page (shown in Exhibit 4-1) stores such information as a contact's company name, address, phone number, and e-mail address. The Details page stores business information, such as the contact's manager and department; and personal information, such as the person's birthday and anniversary.

- **Insert:** Contains controls to insert additional information about or related to the contact. You can attach files, business cards, and signatures. You can also insert pictures, charts, and hyperlinks.

- **Format Text:** Contains controls to format text entered into the Notes area for a contact.

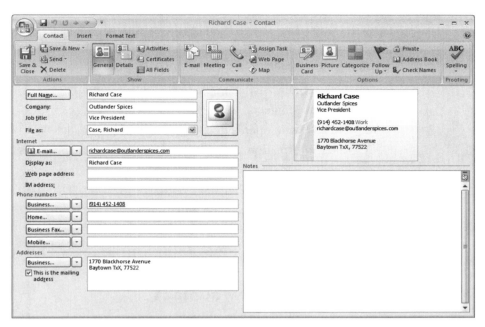

Exhibit 4-1: A sample Contact window

Do it!

A-1:   Exploring the Contacts folder

Here's how	Here's why
1 Activate Contacts	(Click Contacts in the Navigation pane.) Notice that no entries appear in the Folder Contents list. By default, the Contacts folder is empty until you add entries.
2 Observe the Standard toolbar	Contact-specific buttons appear on the Standard toolbar.
3 Observe the buttons on the right side of the Folder Contents list	When you click any letter, the contact names beginning with the selected letter appear in the Folder Contents list, if the list is not empty.

Adding a contact

Explanation There are two ways you can add a contact to your Contacts list. You can add a new contact by using the new Contact window, or you can add a contact from a received e-mail message header.

To add a new contact by using the new Contact window:

1 Activate Contacts.

2 Click New to open a new Contact window.

3 Enter information about the contact, such as the person's name, address, telephone number, and fax number.

4 In the Actions group, click Save & Close.

To add a contact from a received e-mail message, open or preview the message in the Reading pane. In the message header, right-click the sender's e-mail address and choose Add to Outlook Contacts from the shortcut menu. In the Contact window, enter any additional information and click Save & Close.

Do it!   ## A-2: Adding a new contact

Here's how	Here's why
1 Click **New**	(The New button is on the Standard toolbar.) To open a new Contact window.
Maximize the window	Notice that the insertion point appears in the Full Name box.
2 In the Full Name box, enter **Richard Case**	To specify the name of the contact.
Press (TAB)	To move the insertion point to the next box. The name of the contact appears automatically in the format "last name, first name" in the File as list. This setting controls how Outlook saves the contact information for future reference. Outlook files the contact information alphabetically by the last name.
3 In the Company box, enter **Western Spice Retailers**	To specify the contact's company name. In this case, Western Spice Retailers is a customer of Outlander Spices.
Press (TAB)	To move the insertion point to the next box.
4 In the Job title box, enter **Senior Buyer**	To specify the contact's job title.

5 Under Addresses, click as shown

Addresses

Business...

☐ This is the mailing address

A menu appears. You can choose one of the three types of addresses—Business, Home, and Other—by clicking the drop-down arrow near the Business button. By default, Business is selected.

Press ⌷ESC⌷   To hide the menu.

6 Under Addresses, click
   Business   To open the Check Address dialog box.

   Enter business address details as
   shown

Address details

Street:	1770 Blackhorse Avenue
City:	Baytown
State/Province:	TX
ZIP/Postal code:	77522
Country/Region:	United States of America ▾

   Click **OK**   To close the Check Address dialog box. The
                                              option "This is the mailing address" is checked.

7 Observe the text boxes under
   Phone numbers

Phone numbers

Business...	▾	
Home...	▾	
Business Fax...	▾	
Mobile...	▾	

                                              There are four boxes for phone numbers:
                                              Business, Home, Business Fax, and Mobile.

8 Under Phone numbers, click
   Business

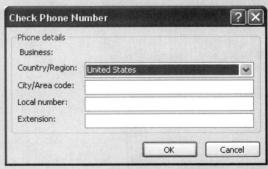

                                              To open the Check Phone Number dialog box.

9 In the Country/Region list, verify that United States is selected	This list is used to specify the region or country.
In the City/Area code box, enter **914**	To specify the area code.
In the Local number box, enter **452-1408**	To specify the telephone number.
Click **OK**	
	To close the Check Phone Number dialog box. The phone number appears in the box near Business under Phone numbers in the Contact window.
10 In the Show group on the Ribbon, click **Details**	Here, you can enter details such as the contact's manager, department, birthday, and anniversary.
In the Department box, enter **Marketing**	
11 In the Actions group on the Ribbon, click **Save & Close**	
	To save the contact information and close the Contact window. Notice that Case, Richard is listed as a contact in the Folder Contents list.
12 Display your Inbox	Activate Mail and click Inbox.
Select a message from your partner	Choose one that isn't signed or encrypted.
Right-click your partner's e-mail address	In the message header displayed in the Reading Pane.
Choose **Add to Outlook Contacts**	To open a new Contact window displaying your partner's contact information.
Click **Save & Close**	

Modifying and saving contacts

Explanation

After creating a contact item, you might need to change the information. For example, if your client's address changes, you need to update the address accordingly. You can modify a contact and save the changes as the current contact or you can modify the contact and save the changes as a new contact. You can also add items to your contacts such as important documents, business cards, or messages.

Modifying a contact

You can easily modify a contact. To edit a contact, double-click it to open the Contact window. Then edit the information and save the contact. This saves the changes to the current contact file.

You can also modify a contact and save it as a new contact. Here's how:

1   Open the contact you want to modify and save it as a new contact.

2   Make your modifications.

3   Click the Office button and choose Save As.

4   Enter a name for the file.

5   From the Save as type list, select vCard Files and then click Save.

6   Click the Office button and choose Close to close the current contact. Do not save the changes.

7   Choose File, Import and Export.

8   Select Import a vCard file and click Next.

9   Locate and select the vCard file; then click Open.

Do it!

A-3:   Modifying a contact

Here's how	Here's why
1 Activate Contacts	
2 Double-click **Case, Richard**	To open the details of Richard Case in the Contact window. You need to change the job title for this contact, and add the e-mail address.
3 In the E-mail box, enter **richard_case@hotmail.com**	To specify the e-mail address. You can add a maximum of three e-mail addresses.
4 Edit the Job title box to read **Vice President**	To change the job title.
5 Save the contact information	

Contacts   Cas

Case, Richard

Richard Case
Western Spice Retailers
Vice President
Marketing

+1 (914) 452-1408 Work
richard_case@hotmail.com
1770 Blackhorse Avenue
Baytown, TX 77522

(Click Save & Close.) Notice that the changes are reflected in the contact information in the Folder Contents list.

6 Open the contact Richard Case	You'll modify and create a new contact now that Richard Case is also the CEO for Outlander Spices.
7 Edit the Company box to read **Outlander Spices**	
8 Edit the Job title box to read **CEO**	
9 Edit the e-mail address to read **richardcase@outlanderspices.com**	

10 Click 📇	You'll save the modified contact as a vCARD file and then import it into your Contacts.
Click **Save As**	
Navigate to the current unit folder	To save the vCARD file.
In the File name box, enter **Richard Case 2**	
From the Save as type list, select **vCard Files**	
Click **Save**	
11 Click 📇	
Choose **Close**	
Click **No**	You do not want to save the changes to the current contact.
12 Choose **File**, **Import and Export...**	To open the Import and Export Wizard dialog box. You'll now import the modified contact.
Select **Import a VCARD file**	
Click **Next**	
Navigate to the current unit folder	If necessary.
Select the Richard Case 2 file	
Click **Open**	

Attach items to contacts

Explanation

You can attach files and Outlook items such as messages and appointments to a contact.

To attach a file, such as a Word document or Excel worksheet, open the contact. Activate the Insert tab and click the Attach File button in the Include group. Select the file you want to attach and click Insert. The link to the file will appear in the Notes section. You can view the file by double-clicking its icon.

You can also attach Outlook items, such as a message, another contact, or an appointment, to a contact. To attach an Outlook item:

1 Open the Contact.
2 Activate the Insert tab and click the Attach Item button in the Include group.
3 From the Look in list, select the folder containing the Outlook item.
4 Select the item in the Items list and click OK.

Do it!

A-4: Attaching items to a contact

Here's how	Here's why
1 Open your Richard Case contact	(Double-click the first Richard Case contact.) You'll attach a Word document to the contact.
2 Activate the Insert tab	
3 Click **Attach File**	To open the Insert File dialog box.
Navigate to the current unit folder	
Select **Richard Case Bio**	
Click **Insert**	Notes — Richard Case Bio.docx
	An icon for the attached Word document appears in the Notes section.
4 Activate the Contact tab	You'll save and close the contact.
Click **Save & Close**	
5 Activate Mail	
6 Create and send a new message addressed to your partner with the subject **Richard Case Bio**	
7 Check for new messages	
8 Activate Contacts	

9	Open the first Richard Case contact	You'll attach a message to the Richard Case contact.
10	Activate the Insert tab	
11	Click **Attach Item**	To open the Insert Item dialog box.
	From the Look in: list, select **Inbox**	If necessary.
	From the Items list, select the Richard Case Bio message	
	Under Insert as, verify that Attachment is selected	
	Click **OK**	

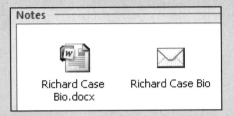

The message icon appears in the Notes area.

12	Save and close the contact

Adding contacts from the same company

Explanation

Several of your contacts might work for the same company. For these contacts, most of the information—such as the company name, the phone number, and the address—will be the same.

You can save the time and effort spent in entering information for these contacts by selecting a contact from the same company and then choosing Actions, New Contact from Same Company. When you create a contact with this command, the company-related information appears automatically in the Contact window, as shown in Exhibit 4-2. You can then enter other details, such as the name and job title.

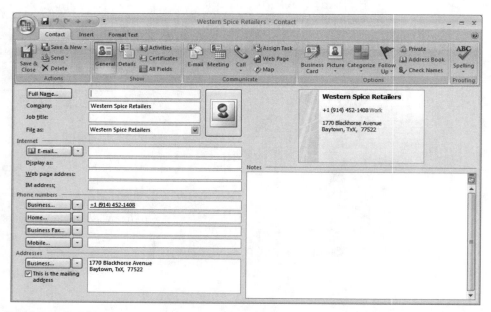

Exhibit 4-2: The new Contact window filled in with company information

Do it!

A-5: Adding a contact from the same company

Here's how	Here's why
1 Verify that Case, Richard is selected	In the Folder Contents list.
2 Choose **Actions, New Contact from Same Company**	You'll add another contact from Western Spice Retailers. The name of the company, the business address, and the business phone number appear automatically in the Contact window, as shown in Exhibit 4-2.
3 In the Full Name box, enter **Michael Gos**	To specify the name of the contact.
In the Job title box, enter **Assistant Buyer**	To specify the job title of the contact.
Save and close the contact information	Michael Gos appears as a contact in the Folder Contents list.

Send and save contacts

Explanation   If a colleague needs the information for one of your contacts, instead of typing a contact's information into a message, simply attach the contact to an e-mail message. Create a new message and click Attach Item. From the Look in list, select Contacts. Under Items, select the contact you want to attach, and then click OK. You can save a contact attachment as a contact record from an e-mail message. To do so:

1   Open the message.

2   Double-click the contact attachment. The Contact window containing the contact's information will appear.

3   Click Save & Close to save the contact in your Contacts.

Do it!   **A-6:   Sending and saving contacts**

Here's how	Here's why
1 Create another contact from Western Spice Retailers named **<xx>Jill Smith**	Where <xx> is your partner's number.
2 Save the contact	
3 Activate Mail	You'll send the Jill Smith contact to your partner.
4 Create a new message addressed to your partner with the subject **<xx>Jill Smith Contact**	
5 Click **Attach Item**	(In the Include group.) You'll attach the Jill Smith Contact to the message.
Under Look in:, select **Contacts**	
Under Items: select **Smith, <xx>Jill**	
Click **OK**	
6 Send the message	
7 Check for new messages	
8 Open the <yy>Jill Smith Contact message from your partner	
9 Double-click **<yy>Jill Smith**	The <yy>Jill Smith Contact window appears.
Click **Save & Close**	To save the contact in your Contacts and close the window.
10 Close the message window	
11 Activate Contacts	Notice the <yy>Jill Smith contact is listed in Contacts.

Contacts folder views

Explanation

Outlook offers several views for each folder. A *view* is the way the data appears in the Folder Contents list. In Contacts, the default view is Business Cards. In this view, you can see the person's name, company information, phone numbers, fax numbers, e-mail address, and the company address for each contact. The other views available for the Contacts folder are shown in Exhibit 4-3.

Exhibit 4-3: Current View in Contacts pane

To change the view for the Contacts folder, select the view you want to use from the Current View list in the Contacts pane. You can also select the desired view from the Current View list on the Advanced toolbar. View names that begin with "By" are the categorized views.

Do it!

A-7: Viewing your contacts

Here's how	Here's why
1 Observe the Folder Contents list	Each contact appears as a business address card. These cards are sorted alphabetically and show a few important details, such as a contact's address and phone numbers.
2 In the Contacts pane, in the Current View list, select **By Company**	Company: Western Spice Retailers (4 items) / Richard Case — Vice President — Western Spice R... / Michael Gos — Assistant Bu... — Western Spice R...
	To display the contact information by company name.
3 Explore the other views	View names preceded with "By" are the categorized views. You'll work with these types of views later in the topic.
4 From the Current View list, select **Address Cards**	To switch to Address Cards view.

Topic B: Distribution lists

This topic covers the following Microsoft Certified Application Specialist exam objectives for Outlook 2007.

#	Objective
1.1.1	Send messages to multiple recipients
	• Distribution list
4.3	**Create and modify distribution lists**
	• Create a new distribution list
	• Add and remove people from distribution lists
	• Update distribution list member information

Creating and using distribution lists

Explanation

When you work in a team, you might need to address multiple messages to the same group of people (such as the other members of your team). For example, suppose that you regularly send an updated price list to all the kiosk managers. To perform this task, you can create a distribution list with the e-mail addresses of all the kiosk managers. A *distribution list* contains several e-mail addresses under a single entry.

You can create distribution lists in the Global Address Book or as contacts in your personal Contacts folder. To create a distribution list in the Global or Outlook Address Books, you must have the necessary permissions and rights.

To create a distribution list in your Contacts folder:

1   Choose File, New, Distribution List to open a new Distribution List window, as shown in Exhibit 4-4.
2   In the Name box, enter the name you want to use for the group.
3   In the Members group on the Ribbon, click Select Members to open the Select Members dialog box.
4   Select a member from the Name list and click Members.
5   Repeat step 4 until all the members are selected and then click OK.
6   In the Actions group, click Save & Close.

If you have multiple members to add, you can select multiple members in step 4 by pressing Control, clicking each member you want to include, and then clicking Members. You also can enter e-mail addresses by typing in the Members box at the bottom of the dialog box. Enter a semicolon (;) after each member you add manually.

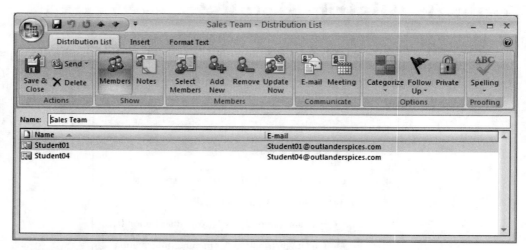

Exhibit 4-4: The Sales Team – Distribution List window

Using a distribution list

One way to send a message to a distribution list is to right-click the distribution list and choosing Create, New Message to Contact. This opens a new Message window. In the To box, the name of the distribution list appears underlined, indicating that it's a valid distribution list. You can then compose and send the message, which will be delivered to everyone in the distribution list.

Another way to send a message to a distribution list is by creating a new e-mail message, and in the To box, entering the name of the distribution list. As you type the first few letters of the distribution list's name, the rest of the name will appear, and you can press Enter to enter it.

Do it! **B-1: Creating and using a distribution list**

Here's how	Here's why
1 Choose **File**, **New**, **Distribution List**	To open a new Distribution List window.
2 In the Name box, enter **Sales Team**	This will be the name of your distribution group.
3 In the Members group on the Ribbon, click **Select Members**	To open the Select Members dialog box. You'll add members to the Sales Team group.
From the Name list, select **Student01**	
Click **Members**	To add the specific student to your distribution list.
4 Add Student04	Select Student04 and click Members.
Click **OK**	To close the Select Members dialog box. The distribution list window appears, as shown in Exhibit 4-4.
5 Click **Save & Close**	Sales Team
	To save the Sales Team distribution list. The Sales Team distribution list appears as a contact in the Folder Contents list.
6 Right-click **Sales Team**	
Choose **Create**, **New Message to Contact**	To... ⊞ Sales Team
	To open a new Message window. Sales Team appears in the To box. The name has been automatically checked and validated against the Global Address Book.
7 Send the message with the subject **Distribution Sales Report**	Enter the subject as Distribution Sales Report and click Send.

Modifying distribution lists

Explanation

After you've created a distribution list, you might need to add or remove members. You also might need to change a member's information, such as by adding a new e-mail address or phone number.

To add a new member to the distribution list:

1   Open the distribution list.
2   In the Members group, click Add New.
3   Enter the display name and e-mail address for the new member and click OK.
4   Click Save and Close.

If you want to add a new member who is already in your address book, then in the distribution list, click Select Members. Select the member, click Members, and then click OK.

To remove a member from the distribution list, open the distribution list. Select the member you want to remove and click Remove in the Members group.

To update member information for a distribution list:

1   Open the distribution list.
2   Double-click the member you want to update.
3   Enter the new information and click Save & Close to return to the distribution list window.
4   Click Save & Close.

To send the updated information to the entire distribution list:

1   Create a new e-mail message, click To, locate and double-click the distribution list, and then click OK.
2   In the Include group, click Attach Item.
3   From the Look in list, select Contacts.
4   From the Items list, select the distribution list, and then click OK.
5   Complete and send the message.

Do it!

B-2:   Modifying a distribution list

Here's how	Here's why
1 Activate Contacts	(If necessary.) You'll add and remove members from the Sales Team distribution list.
2 Double-click the Sales Team distribution list	To open the Sales Team distribution list window.
3 Click **Select Members**	To open the Select Members dialog box. You'll add a new member from your Contacts.
Select **Contacts**	(If necessary.) From the Address Book list.
Select the first **Richard Case** contact	
Click **Members**	
Click **OK**	
4 Select **Student04**	You'll remove this member from the distribution list.
Click **Remove**	In the Members group.
5 Click **Save & Close**	
6 Open the first Richard Case contact	
Edit the e-mail address to be **rcase@westernspices.com**	
Click **Save & Close**	To save the new information.
7 Open the Sales Team distribution list	You'll update the distribution list because Richard Case's e-mail address was changed.
Click **Update Now**	To update the distribution list with information from your Contacts.
Click **Save & Close**	

Topic C: Electronic business cards

This topic covers the following Microsoft Certified Application Specialist exam objectives for Outlook 2007.

#	Objective
4.1.3	Create a contact from an electronic business card
4.2.1	Edit an electronic business card
	• Edit contact information by adding an IM address
	• Specify the information that appears on the business card
	• Format the appearance of a business card
4.2.2	Send an electronic business card to others

Creating and using electronic business cards

Explanation

An electronic business card is a view of a contact that displays specific information for a contact in a form similar to a paper business card. Electronic business cards are VCF files that can be sent to others via e-mail or included in your e-mail signature.

To create an electronic business card, simply create a new contact. When you create a new contact, an electronic business card is also created and associated with the contact.

Do it!

C-1: Creating an electronic business card

Here's how	Here's why
1 Activate Contacts	(If necessary.) You'll create a new contact and electronic business card for yourself.
2 Click **New**	To create a new contact.
3 In the Full Name box, enter your name	
4 Enter **Outlander Spices** as the company	
5 Enter **Marketing Assistant** as your job title	
6 Enter your classroom e-mail address	
7 Under Phone numbers, enter **1-630-555-5555** as your business phone number	

8 Under Addresses, click
   Business

   Enter **123 Main Street,
   Anytown MA 45555**

   Click **OK**

9 Save and close the contact

10 Switch to Business Cards view   Notice that your contact information appears as
                                      a business card.

Modify an electronic business card

Explanation   If you need to make a change to the information that appears in your electronic business card, you'll need to open your contact, make your modifications, and save the contact.

You can also control what information an electronic business card contains. To control what the card includes, open the contact and click Business Card in the Options group to open the Edit Business Card dialog box, shown in Exhibit 4-5.

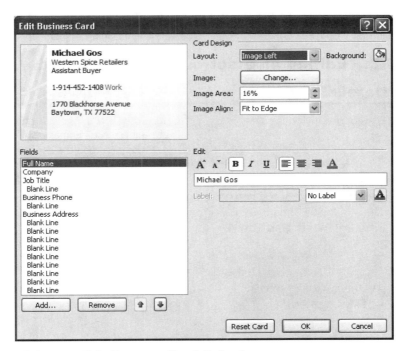

Exhibit 4-5: Edit Business Card dialog box

In the Edit Business Card dialog box, you can make your changes to what content will be displayed by changing the fields that appear on the business card. These fields correspond to the fields in the Contact window. You can change which fields are displayed on your card by adding or removing them from the Fields list:

- To add a new field to the list and display its content on the card, click Add and select from the list of available fields.

- To keep a field from being included with the card, select its field name under Fields and click Remove. If you want to add a field back, all you need to do is click Add and select it from the list.

Moving fields

In an electronic business card, you're not stuck with any particular order of content display. You can move the fields around. To move a field up or down on the electronic business card, select the field in the list, and then click the Move Field Up and Move Field Down buttons at the bottom of the dialog box.

Editing field values

You can also edit the value of a field in the Edit Business Card dialog box. To do this, select the field and edit the value under Edit. Keep in mind that when you edit the value of the field as it appears in the business card, you are also modifying it for the associated contact. If you delete a value for a field, it will be removed from the electronic business card, but it will also be removed from the contact. If you don't want a field displayed on the card, then use the Remove button instead.

Do it!

C-2: Editing an electronic business card

Here's how	Here's why
1 Open your contact	You'll add an instant messaging address to the electronic business card and modify the fields displayed on the card.
2 Next to IM address, enter **Student\<yy\>@msnx.com**	Where \<yy\> is your assigned student number.
3 Click **Business Card**	(In the Options group.) To open the Edit Business Card dialog box. Notice that the IM address appears at the bottom of the card.
4 Under Fields, select **IM Address**	You'll move the IM address so it is under the Work phone number.
Click ⬆ until the IM address is beneath the e-mail address	The instant messaging address should now appear beneath the e-mail address.

5	Click **Add**	To display a menu. You'll add the Department field to the business card.
	Choose **Organization**, **Department**	
	Click [⬆] until the Department field is below Company	
	Under Edit, enter **Marketing**	To set the department to Marketing.
6	Under Fields, click **Department**	You'll delete the department.
	Click **Remove**	
7	Under Fields, select **IM Address**	You'll edit the value for the IM address.
8	Under Edit, change the value for the IM field to **Student\<yy\>@msn.com**	You can edit each value listed in the business card. It is best to keep your edits to correcting small mistakes. Use the Contact form to add new information.
	Edit the text in the Label box to read **IM Address:**	
	Select **Left** from the Label position list	
9	Under Fields, select **E-mail**	
	From the label position list, select **Left**	
	In the Label box, enter **E-mail:**	
10	Under Fields, select **Business Phone**	You'll change the label position so it is to the left of the phone number.
	Edit the label to read **Work:**	Add a colon to the end of the word.
	Select **Left** from the Label position list	
11	Under Fields, select the first **Blank Line** item beneath Business Address	
	Click [⬆]	
12	Click **OK**	Notice the IM address has been updated in the Contact window.
13	Click **Save & Close**	

Design and format an electronic business card

Explanation

You can change the design of an electronic business card and format the text on the business card by using the Edit Business Card dialog box. Open the contact and then click Business Card in the Options group to open the Edit Business Card dialog box, as shown in Exhibit 4-6.

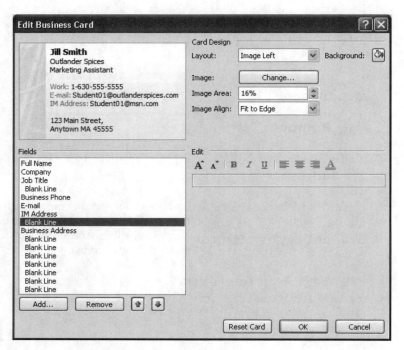

Exhibit 4-6: Edit Business Card dialog box

Changing the design

In the Edit Business Card dialog box, under Card Design, you can change the image; change the image position, area, and alignment; and change the background color.

Select a layout for the image position from the Layout list. You can position the image to be on the left, right, top, or bottom of the card. You can also select Text Only to indicate that no image be used. Select Background Image if you want the image to be located behind the text. With the image in the background, you'll be able to fit more text onto the card.

You can also add your own image instead of using the default one. To do so, click Change next to Image. Locate and select your image and click OK. To change how much area the image occupies, click the up and down arrows next to the Image Area box. Then select the alignment from the Image Align list.

You can also change the background color for your electronic business card. Click the Background button. In the Color dialog box, click the color you want to use and click OK. To specify a custom color, click Define Custom Colors. Enter the RGB values for the color you want or click in the color box to select a color. Click OK to apply the color to your card.

Formatting text on an electronic business card

In the Edit Business Card dialog box, under Edit, you can format content of each field and add labels for fields. You make text changes one line at a time by clicking the field you want to format (either click in the business card mock-up at the top of the dialog box or in the Fields list) and then, under Edit, make the changes you want.

You can use white space to draw attention to important details in your card. To create white space in your electronic business card, either add Blank Line fields or move an existing Blank Line field up or down.

Do it!

C-3: Formatting an electronic business card

Here's how	Here's why
1 Open the Edit Business Card dialog box for your contact	(Open the contact and then click Business Card in the Options group.) You'll change the design of the electronic business card and reformat some of the text.
2 Under Card Design, from the Layout list, select **Image Top**	Notice in the preview that the image is moved to the top of the business card and the address is no longer visible on the card.
3 Click	(The Background Color button.) To open the Color dialog box. You'll change the background to a pale yellow color.
Click the palest yellow color	
Click **OK**	
4 Under Fields, select **Business Phone**	You'll change the label color to red.
Click	(The Label Color button is located to the right of the Label position list.) To open the Color dialog box.
Select the color red and click **OK**	
5 Change the IM Address label color to red	Under Fields, select IM Address. Click the Label Color button, select red, and then click OK.
6 Change the E-mail label to red	
7 Click **OK**	
8 Save and close the contact	The electronic business card now displays the new formatting.

Send an electronic business card

Explanation

After you've created your electronic business card, you can use it to share your contact information with business associates and friends. To share your contact information, send it in an e-mail message.

1 Create a new message.

2 In the Include group, click the Business Card button and select Other Business Cards.

3 Select your card from the list and click OK. The business card appears in the body of the message and a VCF file attachment is added to the Attached box.

4 Send your message.

The attachment is in vCard format, the Internet standard for creating and sharing virtual business cards. Because the file is in vCard format, even people who aren't using Outlook 2007 most likely will be able to easily save the contact information. The attached vCard also contains all of the contact information, and not just the information displayed on the electronic business card.

Do it!

C-4: Sending an electronic business card

Here's how	Here's why
1 Activate Mail	You'll send your electronic business card to your partner.
2 Create a new message addressed to your partner	
Enter **Student<yy> electronic business card** as the subject	
3 Click **Business Card**	In the Include group.
Select **Other Business Cards...**	To open the Insert Business Card dialog box.
4 From the Look in list, select **Contacts**	If necessary.
Select your contact	A preview of the business card appears.
Click **OK**	The electronic business card appears in the message area and the VCF file is attached to the message.
5 Click **Send**	

Create a contact from an electronic business card

Explanation

You can save an electronic business card from an e-mail message to create a new contact. In an open message, right-click the electronic business card and choose Add to Outlook Contacts. A new Contact window appears containing the contact's information. On the Contact tab, click Save & Close to save the contact. If you already have a contact with the same name, Outlook detects the duplicate and prompts you to add the contact as a new contact or to update the information for a selected contact.

The new contact information is now saved in Contacts, and is available in Business Card and other views. You can make changes to the contact information both before and after you save it.

Do it!

C-5:   Creating a contact from an electronic business card

Here's how	Here's why
1 Check for new messages	You'll create a contact from your partner's electronic business card.
2 Open the message from your partner with the subject Student<yy> electronic business card	
3 In the message area, right-click the business card and choose **Add to Outlook Contacts**	A Contact window appears containing the information for the contact. Notice that even though the address is not displayed in the electronic business card, it does appear in the Contact window.
4 Click **Save & Close**	To save the contact.
5 Close the Message window	

Unit summary: Contact management

Topic A   In this topic, you used the Contacts folder to **create** and **edit contacts**. You also added contacts from the same company. Then you used the different **views** by using the Current View list to find messages.

Topic B   In this topic, you created and used **distribution lists**, which make it easier to send a message to multiple recipients. You also added and removed members on a distribution list and updated member information.

Topic C   In this topic, you created and used **electronic business cards**. You sent an electronic business card to a recipient. You formatted an electronic business card. You also created a contact from an electronic business card.

Independent practice activity

In this activity, you'll add new contacts and create a new distribution list. You'll address a new message to a specified distribution list.

1 Add Peter Greenfield's contact information as shown in Exhibit 4-7. Save the contact information.

2 Add **Scott Bates** as a new contact from the same company as Peter Greenfield, and specify his job title as **Marketing Director**. Save the contact information.

3 Create a distribution list with the name **Purchase Team**. Add Student03 and Student05 as members. Save the information.

4 Send a message to Purchase Team with the subject **Requirements** and a brief message of your choice.

5 Add the e-mail address pgreenfield@wonderlandhotels.com to the Peter Greenfield contact.

6 Remove the image from the electronic business card for Peter Greenfield and change the background color to a light blue color.

7 Modify the label for the phone number to be **Phone:** and move it to the left side.

8 Enter **E-mail:** as a label for the e-mail address field and move the label to the left side.

9 Remove +1 from the phone number value.

10 Save and close the business card.

11 Save and close the contact.

Exhibit 4-7: The contact information to be added in step 1 of the Independent practice activity

Review questions

1 What procedure is used to create a new contact?

2 How do you edit an existing contact?

3 Name two ways to change the view in the Contacts folder.

4 How do you create a contact from a received e-mail message?

5 How do you create a new contact that works for the same company as one of your previous contacts?

6 What is the advantage of creating a distribution list?

7 How do you send a message to a distribution list?

8 How do you create an electronic business card?

9 Can you modify the information shown in an electronic business card?

10 How do you send an electronic business card to another person?

11 How do you save an electronic business card received in a message as a contact?

U n i t 5

Tasks

Unit time: 40 minutes

Complete this unit, and you'll know how to:

A Use the Tasks folder and To-Do bar to create, edit, and delete single and recurring tasks; insert a task into a message; and categorize and view your tasks.

B Use the Tasks folder to assign tasks, accept or decline a task request, send a status report, and track the completion of an assigned task.

Topic A: Working with tasks

This topic covers the following Microsoft Certified Application Specialist exam objectives for Outlook 2007.

#	Objective
3.1.1	**Create recurring tasks**
	• Create a task that occurs every Monday for a six-month period beginning the first week in January
3.1.2	**Create a task from a message**
	• Flag the message from Person A as a task and set it to be completed next week
3.1.3	**Set the status, priority, and percent complete of a task**
	• Mark the status of Task A as In Progress, its priority as High, and the percent complete to 50%
	• Mark the status of Task A as Deferred
3.1.4	**Mark a task as complete**
3.1.5	**Mark a task as private**

The Tasks folder and the To-Do bar

Explanation

In Outlook, a *task* is an activity that must be completed within a specified period of time. A task has a current status, which can be In Progress, Not Started, Waiting on someone else, Deferred, or Completed.

You can create tasks and monitor their status in the *To-Do Bar Task list* or the *Tasks folder*. After creating a task, you can also edit or delete it. In addition, you also send a task through e-mail as an attachment.

The To-Do Bar Task list and the Tasks folder store the tasks you need to perform. For example, you might have some tasks that another person has assigned to you. You can view the task by looking at the Task list in the To-Do bar, or you can display the Tasks folder by clicking Tasks in the Navigation pane. A sample Tasks window with tasks is shown in Exhibit 5-1. The list of tasks appears in the Folder Contents list and the same list appears in the Task list on the To-Do bar.

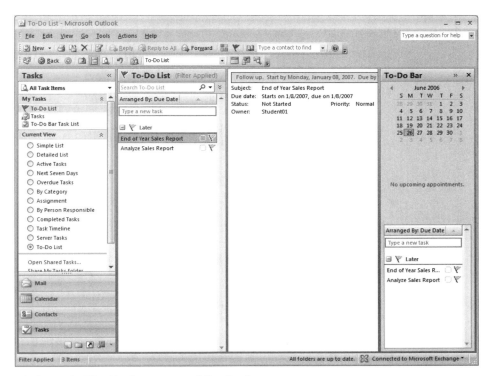

Exhibit 5-1: The Tasks pane and To-Do bar

Do it!

A-1:   Exploring the Tasks folder and To-Do bar

Here's how	Here's why
1 Activate Tasks	Click Tasks in the Navigation pane.
2 Observe the Folder pane	**▼ To-Do List** (Filter Applied) Search To-Do List 🔍 ▼ ⋙ Notice that by default, the folder pane shows the To-Do Bar Task list.
3 Observe the To-Do bar	Arranged By: Due Date ▲ Type a new task There are no items to show in this view. Notice that the Task Input Panel and Task list are located at the bottom of the To-Do bar.
4 Observe the Standard toolbar	Task-specific buttons are now available.
5 Display the Advanced toolbar	If necessary.
6 View the Current View list on the Advanced toolbar	To-Do List ▼ By default, To-Do List is selected.

Creating and deleting tasks

Explanation   There are several ways you can create a task:

- Enter the task into the Task Input Panel on the To-Do bar.
- Choose File, New Task; choose Actions, New Task; or click the New button on the Standard toolbar from the Tasks pane to open a new Task window as shown in Exhibit 5-2. When you create a new task, enter the Start and Due dates. Specify the status and priority of the task, and the percentage of the task that is complete. Then click Save & Close.
- Flag a message to add it to your To-Do Bar Task list. When you receive a message that requires performing a task, click the flag to add it to today's task list. You can also right-click the flag and specify a due date for the task.

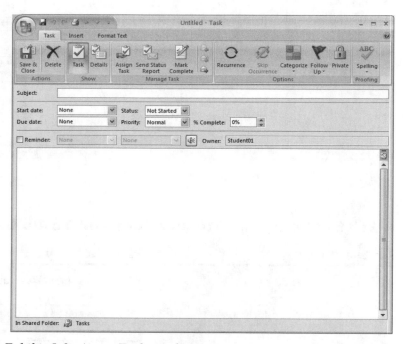

Exhibit 5-2: A new Task window

The Task Input panel

You can quickly create tasks by using the Task Input panel. Click the Task Input panel and enter a subject. By default, the task will be assigned a due date and a start date of Today. Double-click the task to edit its settings.

The new Task window

The Show group on the new Task window's Ribbon contains two buttons: Task and Details. You use the Task button to enter details about a task, such as the subject, start and end dates, status, and priority. You use the Details button to enter details such as the total work estimated, the actual time taken, and expenses incurred to complete the task.

To delete a task, select the task in the To-Do Bar Task list and click the Delete button on the Standard toolbar.

Do it!

A-2:   Creating and deleting tasks

Here's how	Here's why
1 Click **New**	(The New button is on the Standard toolbar.) To open a new Task window. You'll create a new task: analyzing a sales report. The sales report has to be analyzed, and the feedback has to be sent within two days.
2 In the Subject box, enter **Analyze Sales Report**	To specify the subject of the task.
3 Click the arrow near the Start date list	To display the Date Navigator.
Click **Today**	Due today. Subject: Analyze Sales Report
	To specify the start date of the task. Notice that the InfoBar indicates that the task is due today.
4 Click the arrow near the Due date list	To display the Date Navigator.
Select the date two days ahead of the current date	Due in 2 days. Subject: Analyze Sales Report
	(From the Date Navigator.) To specify the due date. The InfoBar now indicates that the task is due in two days.
5 From the Status list, select **In Progress**	To specify that this task is in progress. The other options available in this list are Not Started, Completed, Waiting on someone else, and Deferred.
6 From the Priority list, select **High**	To specify the importance of the task. The other options available in this list are Normal and Low. By default, Normal priority is assigned to a task.
7 Edit the % Complete box to read **50%**	To specify the percentage of the task that is completed.
8 Check **Reminder**	To set a reminder for the task.
In the Reminder date list, verify the due date	This indicates the date on which the reminder should appear.
9 From the Reminder time list, select **11:00 AM**	To specify the time when the reminder should appear.

10	Click **Save & Close**	(The Save & Close button is in the Actions group on the Ribbon.) To save the task and close the new Task window. The Analyze Sales Report task appears in the Folder Contents list.
11	Activate Mail	You'll create a task from a message.
12	Create a new message addressed to your partner	
	Enter the subject as **<xx>: Meeting Agenda**	In place of <xx>, enter your partner's number.
	Send the message to your partner	
13	Check for new messages	
14	Right-click the message flag and choose **Next Week**	To flag the message from your partner as a task and set it to be completed next week.
15	Activate Tasks	Notice the new task appears in both your To-Do bar and the Task list under the Next Week section.
16	From the Current View list, select **Detailed List**	(In the Tasks pane or on the Advanced toolbar.) To see a more detailed view of the tasks.
17	In the Task Input Panel, enter a task with the subject **Sales Task**	(On the To-Do bar.) Notice that the task appears with today as its due date.
18	Click **Sales Task**	(In the Folder Contents list.) To select the task with the subject Sales task. You'll delete this task.
	Delete the task	Click the Delete button on the Standard toolbar.

Editing tasks

Explanation

As you work on your tasks, the status or the percentage completed might change. To reflect these changes, you'll need to edit the task information. You can edit information about a task, such as the status, the due date, and the percentage of completion. You can also mark tasks as private.

To edit a task:

1   Open the task.
2   Make the changes you want to the due date, status, priority, and percent complete.
3   Click Save & Close.

Marking a task as private

You can mark a task as private to prevent other people from accessing the details of the task. To ensure that other people cannot read the items that you mark as private, do not grant them Read permission to your Tasks folder. Use the private status only when you share folders with people whom you trust. To mark a task as private, open the task and click Private in the Options group; then save the task.

Do it!

A-3:   Editing a task

Here's how	Here's why
1 In the Folder Contents list, double-click **Analyze Sales Report**	To open the task with the subject Analyze Sales Report. You'll edit the task. The deadline for completing the analysis of the sales report has been extended by a day. You'll edit the task to update this information.
2 From the Status list, select **Deferred**	To specify that the task is delayed or postponed.
3 Specify the due date as three days ahead of the current date	(Display the Date Navigator in the Due date list and select the date three days ahead of the current date.) To change the due date. The Reminder list reflects the change in the due date.
4 Click **Private**	In the Options group on the Ribbon.) To mark the task as private.
5 Save and close the task	The task changes are reflected in the Folder Contents list.

Recurring tasks

A *recurring task* is a task that needs to be performed on a regular basis. To create a recurring task, you need to specify the pattern in which the task recurs. For example, you can specify a task for the first Monday of every month or the fourth Wednesday of April. This is called the *recurrence pattern*, which can be annual, monthly, weekly, or daily. You also need to specify the *range of recurrence*, which indicates the start and end period of the recurring task.

To create a recurring task:

1   Open a new Task window.
2   Enter the necessary information.
3   On the Ribbon, in the Options group, click Recurrence to open the Task Recurrence dialog box.
4   Specify the options for the recurrence pattern.
5   Click OK.
6   Click Save & Close.

Do it!

A-4:   Adding a recurring task

Here's how	Here's why
1 Create a task with the subject **Generate Sales Report**	Open a new Task window, and enter the subject "Generate Sales Report."
	You need to send a sales report to a manager every Monday for a six-month period beginning the first week of January. So, instead of creating a task every week, you'll create a recurring task.
Specify the due date as the last Monday in June	From the Due date list, display the Date Navigator, and select the date.
	If the InfoBar displays a message indicating the task is overdue, ignore the message.
Specify the start date as the first Monday in January	From the Start date list, display the Date Navigator, and select the date.
2 On the Ribbon, in the Options group, click **Recurrence**	To open the Task Recurrence dialog box.
3 Under Recurrence pattern, select **Weekly**	(If necessary.) To specify that this task has to be performed every week.
Select **Recur every 1 week(s) on**	
Check **Monday**	

4 Examine the options under Range of recurrence	You can specify the start and end dates of the recurrence period. You specify the start date in the Start list. By default, no end date is selected. If you know the number of occurrences, then use the second option to specify that number. If the recurring task ends on a specific date, use the third option.
From the Start list, verify that the first Monday in January is selected	
Select **End by**	
From the End by list, select the last Monday in June	
5 Click **OK**	To close the Task Recurrence dialog box and save the Task Recurrence settings. The InfoBar summarizes the details of the recurring task.
6 Save the task	
	The task is marked with a recurring task icon in the Folder Contents list and in the To-Do Bar Task list.
Click **Dismiss All**	(If necessary.) To close the Reminder window if it appears to remind you of the deadline.

Marking tasks complete

Explanation   When you complete a task, you change the status to Complete. When you do so, Outlook marks the task as completed. There are several ways to mark a task complete:

- Open the task and enter "100%" in the % Complete box.
- Open the task and select Completed from the Status list.
- In the Folder Contents list or the To-Do Bar Task list, right-click the task and choose Mark Complete from the shortcut menu.
- In the Folder Contents list, in Simple List view, check the check box next to the task name.

A completed task is indicated in the Folder Contents list by a strikethrough line. A completed task is not displayed in the To-Do Bar Task list.

A-5: Marking a task as completed

Here's how	Here's why
1 Open a new Task window	
Specify the subject as **My task**	
Specify the start date as the current date	From the Date Navigator in the Start date list, select the current date. Notice that the Due date is also changed to the current date.
2 Save the task	Notice that the task appears in the Folder Contents list and the To-Do Bar Task list.
3 Open the task with the subject My task	(Double-click My task in the Folder Contents list.) Notice that the Status box displays Not Started.
4 Edit the % Complete box to read **25%**	
Press (TAB)	The Status box now displays In Progress.
5 Edit the % Complete box to read **100%**	To mark the task as completed.
Deselect the box	(Click any other box.) The Status box displays Completed.
6 Save the task	
7 View the completed task	

(In the Folder Contents list.) The task is dimmed and appears with a strikethrough line. Notice that the task no longer appears in the To-Do Bar Task list.

Attaching tasks to messages

Explanation

You can attach existing Outlook items, such as notes, tasks, or appointments, to a message. This saves the time spent in retyping the information into the message. For example, while sending a task status report to your manager, instead of creating a new message, you can attach the task to the message or right-click the task and choose Forward from the shortcut menu.

To insert a task into a message:

1 Open a new Message window and address the message.
2 Click Attach Item to open the Insert Item dialog box.
3 From the Look in list, select Tasks.
4 From the Items list, select the task you want to insert into the message.
5 Click OK.

Do it!   ## A-6: Attaching a task to a message

Here's how	Here's why
1 Activate Mail	
2 Create a new message and address it to your partner	
Enter the subject **<xx>: Task Progress**	(In place of <xx>, use your partner's number.) You'll insert a task into the message. By inserting the task into a message, you send the details without assigning the task to the recipient.
In the message area, enter **For your review.**	
Press (↵ ENTER)	To move to the next line.
3 Click **Attach Item**	(In the Include group on the Ribbon.) To open the Insert Item dialog box.
4 From the Look in list, select **Tasks**	
5 From the Items list, select **Analyze Sales Report**	
Click **OK**	To close the Insert Item dialog box. The selected appointment appears as an attachment in the message.
6 Send the message	
7 Check your messages	To receive a message with the attached task from your partner.

Task views

Explanation

Views are used to arrange and manage tasks. Outlook provides several views for tasks, such as Active Tasks and Overdue Tasks. Each view displays tasks in a specific way. For example, Active Tasks view shows you all of the current tasks. You can also view tasks by the person responsible and by completion date.

To switch to a different view, you select it from the Current View list, as shown in Exhibit 5-3, in the Tasks pane or on the Advanced toolbar.

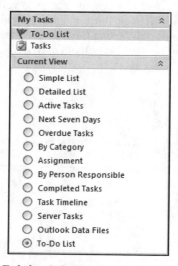

Exhibit 5-3: Task views

Do it!

A-7: Viewing tasks

Here's how	Here's why
1 Activate Tasks	
2 From the Current View list, select **Active Tasks**	To view the current tasks.
3 Explore the other views	
4 Switch to Simple List view	(In the Current View list, select Simple List.) To select the default view for Tasks.

Topic B: Managing tasks

This topic covers the following Microsoft Certified Application Specialist exam objectives for Outlook 2007.

#	Objective
3.2.1	**Assign tasks to others**
	• Assign Task A to Person B
3.2.2	**Respond to an assigned task**
	• Decline Task A and send a message to the person who assigned you the task explaining why you must decline
	• Accept Task A
3.2.3	**Send a status report on an assigned task**
	• Send a Status Report to the task owner

Assigning tasks to others

Explanation

If you're working on a team project, you might need to assign a task to someone else on the team. It might be a task that you cannot finish or one that is more suited to another person. You can create the task and then assign it to someone else by sending a task request. A *task request* is sent in an e-mail message asking the recipient to complete the task. The recipient can accept or decline a task request. If the recipient accepts the task, it's added to the recipient's task list, and the recipient becomes the new owner of the task.

When you assign a task, you might want to track its status. You can do this by keeping an updated copy of the task in your task list and by asking for a status report when the task is completed.

You can also keep a project team updated on your tasks. While you are working on a task, you can send a status report to team members.

To assign a task:

1 Open a new Task window and enter the task subject.
2 In the Manage Task group on the Ribbon, click the Assign Task button.
3 In the To box, enter the e-mail address of the person to whom you want to assign the task.
4 If you want to keep a copy of the task, check Keep an updated copy of this task on my task list.
5 To be notified when the recipient marks the task completed, check Send me a status report when this task is complete.
6 Click Send.

Do it!

B-1: Assigning a task

Here's how	Here's why
1 Create a new task with the subject **<xx>: Update Sales Web site**	(In place of <xx>, use your partner's number.) You'll assign the task of updating a Sales Web site to your partner because you want your partner to complete it.
2 Display the Date Navigator in the Due date list	
3 Click as shown	

◀ February 2007 ▶

S	M	T	W	T	F	S
28	29	30	31	1	2	3
4	5	6	7	8	9	10
11	12	13	14	15	16	17
18	19	20	21	22	23	24
25	26	27	28	1	2	3
4	5	6	7	8	9	10

[Today]   [None]

	To display the calendar for the next month.
Select the last Tuesday of the month	(From the calendar.) To specify it as the due date.
4 From the Start date list, select the first Tuesday of the next month	(Display the calendar for next month, and select the first Tuesday.) To specify the start date.
Clear **Reminder**	If necessary.
5 Click **Details**	(In the Show group on the Ribbon.) To view the Details options.
Edit the Total work box to read **200 hours**	To specify the total time needed for the task.
6 Click **Assign Task**	(The Assign Task button is in the Manage Task group on the Ribbon.) The To box is added to the Task window. The InfoBar informs you that the message has not been sent.
Address the message to your partner	
Verify that Keep an updated copy of this task on my task list is checked	You want to keep a copy of this task. When the assignee accepts the task, the task will be moved to the assignee's Tasks folder, and you'll retain a copy of it.
7 Verify that Send me a status report when this task is complete is checked	To specify that you want to receive a message when the task is completed.
8 Click **Send**	To send the task request message to your partner.
9 Check your messages	To receive the task request message from your partner.

Accepting or declining assigned tasks

Explanation   If you send a task request to someone and he or she accepts it, the task is no longer yours. The recipient becomes the temporary owner of the task. When the recipient accepts the task, a message appears in your Inbox stating that the task request has been accepted and ownership passes to the person who accepted the task.

To accept a task request:

1   Open the task request message.
2   Click Accept.
3   Send a message that informs the sender that you are accepting the task.

When you accept a task, it will appear in your To-Do Bar Task list.

To decline a task request:

1   Open the task request message.
2   Click Decline.
3   Send a message that informs the sender that you are declining the tasks.

When a task is declined, the task's creator receives a message stating that the task request has been declined. To become the owner of the declined task, open the task and click Return to Task List in the Manage Task group on the Ribbon.

Delegating assigned tasks

There might be occasions when you are assigned a task that someone else is better suited to handle. In that case, you can *delegate,* or send, the task to someone else. When the recipient accepts the task, he or she owns the task.

To delegate a task:

1   Open the task request that you want to delegate.
2   Click Assign Task in the Manage Tasks group on the Ribbon.
3   In the To box, enter the new recipient's name.
4   Check, or clear, the desired option to keep a copy of the task in your Tasks folder and to receive a status report when the task is complete.
5   Click Send.

Do it!

B-2: Accepting and declining a task request

Here's how	Here's why
1 Open the Inbox folder	(If necessary.) Activate the Mail pane, and click Inbox.
2 Open the <yy>: Update Sales Web site task request	(Where <yy> is your student number.) Double-click the task request.
3 Click **Accept**	The Accept button is in the Respond group on the Ribbon.
4 Verify that Send the response now is selected	
Click **OK**	To accept the task and notify the sender that you are accepting the task.
5 Observe the Tasks folder	To verify that the task now appears in your Tasks folder.
6 Create a new task with the subject **<xx>: Sales meeting agenda**	
Click **Assign Task**	You'll assign the task to your partner.
Address and send the task to your partner	
7 Activate Mail	
Check for new messages	You'll receive the Sales meeting agenda task assignment from your partner.
8 Open the <yy>: Sales meeting agenda task	
Click **Decline**	To decline the task.
Select **Edit the response before sending**	To be able to enter a message about why you are declining the task.
Click **OK**	
9 In the message area, enter **I will be on vacation next week.**	
Click **Send**	

10 Check for task response messages	You'll receive a task response message that indicates your partner declined the task.

Sending a task status report

Explanation

When a task is assigned to you, the sender of the task request will be interested to know about the status of the task. You can send a task status report to the sender. The task status report contains task details, such as the status and the percentage completed.

To send a task status report:

1 Activate Tasks.
2 Switch to By Person Responsible view.
3 Open the assigned task.
4 Update the task's status and percent complete.
5 Click Details and enter any additional information about the task.
6 Click Send Status Report to open the Message window.
7 Send the report e-mail message.

Do it!

B-3: Sending a task status report

Here's how	Here's why
1 Activate Tasks	If necessary.
2 Switch to By Person Responsible view	In the Current View list, select By Person Responsible.
3 Open the <yy>: Update Sales Web site task	To view the assigned task.
4 Change the Status to **In Progress**	To update the assigned task.
5 Change the % Complete to **50%**	
6 Click **Details**	On the Ribbon, in the Show group.
Edit the Actual work box to read **100 hours**	
7 Click **Send Status Report**	(On the Ribbon, in the Manage Task group.) To open the Message window.
8 Send the report	
9 Click **Save & Close**	To save and close the task window.
10 Check for new messages	To receive your partner's status report.

Tracking a task

Explanation

You might want to receive a confirmation when an assigned task is completed. You track the completion of assigned tasks by using the "Send me a status report when this task is complete" option.

To track a completed task:

1 Create a new task.
2 Assign the task.
3 Check "Send me a status report when this task is complete."
4 Send the task request.

When the task is marked completed by the recipient, you'll receive an e-mail notification.

Do it!

B-4: Tracking an assigned task

Here's how	Here's why
1 Activate Tasks	
2 Open the <yy>: Update Sales Web site task	To view the assigned task.
3 Change the Status to **Completed**	The % Complete box changes to 100%.
4 Close the Task window	
5 Activate Mail	
Click **Send/Receive**	To send and receive the final status report.

Unit summary: Tasks

Topic A

In this topic, you learned that an Outlook **task** is an activity that must be completed in a specified period of time. You used the **To-Do Bar Task list** or Task window to **add** and edit a task. Next, you created a **recurring task** by specifying the recurrence pattern and the range of recurrence. You marked a task as completed and inserted a task into a message. You also learned how to use the different **Task views** by using the Current View list.

Topic B

In this topic, you learned how to **assign** a task to another person. You also learned about accepting, declining, and delegating **task requests**. In addition, you sent a **status report** for an assigned task. You also **tracked** the completion of an assigned task.

Independent practice activity

In this activity, you'll create a task and modify it to be a recurring task. You'll assign a task, and track its completion. You'll also accept a task request, and mark it as completed.

1 Create a task with the subject **Prepare Web usage report**. Specify the start date as the first working day of the next month, and specify the due date as ten days after the start date.

2 Save and close the task.

3 Change Task view to Detailed List.

4 Edit the new task to make it a recurring task. Specify the Recurrence pattern as weekly. The task must recur every Wednesday.

5 Assign the task to your partner. Track the completion of the task.

6 Accept the task request from your partner.

7 Mark the task as completed.

Review questions

1 What is the procedure to create a new task?

2 How can you assign a task to someone else?

3 Who is allowed to edit a task?

4 Which of the following is the term that Outlook uses to describe a task that needs to be performed on a regular basis?

   A Scheduled

   B Repeating

   C Recurring

   D Frequent

5 Name two ways to mark a task complete.

6 True or false? When a task is marked complete, it displays in the Folder Contents list and the To-Do Bar Task list with a strikethrough line.

7 Which button on the Message window's Ribbon is used to insert a task into a message?

8 When a task request is declined, who owns the task?

9 Describe the procedure for sending a status report on a task.

Unit 6

Appointments and events

Unit time: 50 minutes

Complete this unit, and you'll know how to:

A Use the Calendar to set up and view single and recurring appointments.

B Modify, delete, and restore appointments.

C Change the Calendar view to Day, Week, or Month view and modify the work week.

D Add multi-day events, annual events, and holidays to the Calendar.

Topic A: Creating and sending appointments

This topic covers the following Microsoft Certified Application Specialist exam objectives for Outlook 2007.

#	Objective
2.1.1	Create a one-time appointment, meeting, or event
2.1.2	Create a recurring appointment, meeting, or event
2.1.3	Create an appointment, meeting, or event from an e-mail message
2.1.4	Create an appointment, meeting, or event from a task
2.1.5	Mark an appointment, meeting, or event as private

The Outlook Calendar interface

Explanation

You can use Outlook's Calendar to set up appointments and organize your schedules. You can select how much of your schedule you want to view at once. The Calendar interface consists of the Calendar pane, the Calendar view, the Daily Task list, and the To-Do bar, as shown in Exhibit 6-1. There are three Calendar views: Day view, Week view, or Month view. By default, the Day view is selected, which displays the selected day in one-hour increments.

The Daily Task list appears in the Day and Week views, as shown in Exhibit 6-1. This list displays your tasks for the selected day or for each day of the selected week.

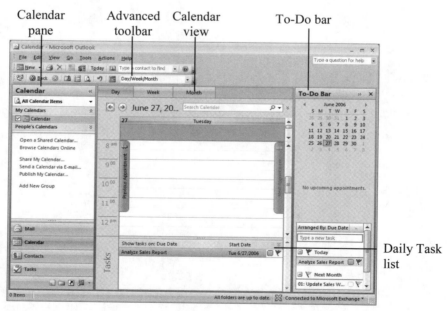

Exhibit 6-1: The Calendar interface

Do it!

A-1:   Exploring the Calendar

Here's how	Here's why
1 Activate the Calendar	Click Calendar in the Navigation pane.
2 Observe the Standard toolbar	Calendar-specific buttons are now available.
3 Display the Advanced toolbar	(If necessary.) Choose View, Toolbars, Advanced.
Observe the Current View list on the Advanced toolbar	`Day/Week/Month  ▾`
	It shows Day/Week/Month as the default view.
4 Observe the Calendar view	It shows the current day divided into one-hour increments. Notice that the Daily Task list displays at the bottom of the view.
5 Display the To-Do Bar	(If necessary.) Select View, To-Do Bar, Normal.
6 Observe the Date Navigator	(The Date Navigator is on the To-Do bar.) By default, it shows the dates for the current month. Use the arrows on the Date Navigator to move to other months.

Creating appointments

Explanation

There are several ways to create an appointment:

- By using a new Appointment window, as shown in Exhibit 6-2.
- By using the Click to Add Appointment feature.

To open a new Appointment window, choose File, New, Appointment, or activate the Calendar and click the New button on the Standard toolbar.

In the Appointment window, you specify the subject, location, time, and duration of the appointment. Notice that an appointment does not include a recipient list. If you need to add attendees, then you want to create a meeting request. You can specify several options by using the Options group on the Ribbon. You can specify your availability status by using the Show As list. An appointment can have an availability status of Free, Tentative, Busy, or Out of Office. Each status has a color associated with it. You can also set a reminder for the appointment. To save the appointment, click Save and Close. After you create and save an appointment, it appears in your Calendar view and also in the To-Do bar.

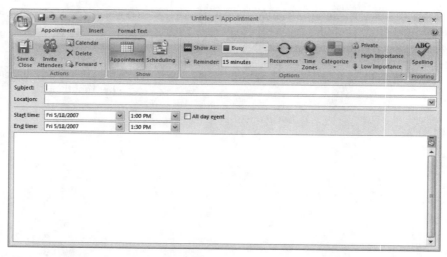

Exhibit 6-2: A sample Appointment window

Click to Add Appointment

You can quickly add an appointment to your schedule using the Click to Add Appointment feature. Simply point to the time or date on the calendar grid. When "Click to Add Appointment" appears, as shown in Exhibit 6-3, click once, type the subject for the appointment, and press Enter.

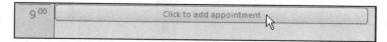

Exhibit 6-3: Click to Add Appointment

Creating appointments from messages and tasks

You can also create appointments from messages and tasks. To do so, click the Folder List icon in the Navigation pane. Then, drag the message or task to the Calendar folder. When the Appointment window appears, configure and save the appointment.

Marking an appointment as private

You can mark an appointment as private to prevent other people from accessing the details of your appointments, contacts, or tasks. To ensure that other people cannot read the items that you mark as private, do not grant them Read permission to your Calendar, Contacts, or Tasks folders. Use the private designation only when you share folders with people whom you trust. To mark an appointment as private, open the appointment and click Private in the Options group.

Do it!

A-2: Setting up an appointment

Here's how	Here's why
1 Click 🗒 New ▾	To open a new Appointment window.
2 In the Subject box, enter **Appointment with Jack**	To specify the subject of the appointment.
3 In the Location box, enter **Conference Room**	To specify the location of the appointment.
4 From the Start time list, select the date for the day after tomorrow	To specify the start date for the appointment.
From the list near the Start time list, select **10:00 AM**	To specify the start time for the appointment. Notice that in the End time list, the end date is the same as the start day by default.
Observe the list near the End time list	The end time appears as 30 minutes from the start time. By default, the time interval is 30 minutes.
5 Observe the Reminder value	(In the Options group on the Ribbon.) This indicates that you have set a reminder for the appointment.
From the Reminder list, select **10 minutes**	You'll receive an audible and visual notification 10 minutes before the appointment.
Observe the text area under the End time lists	You can enter any additional comments here.

6 Click **Private**	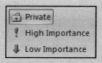
	(In the Options group on the Ribbon.) To mark the appointment as private.
7 Click **Save & Close**	To save the appointment and close the Appointment window. Notice that the Next Appointment button in the Calendar view becomes active.
8 Observe the To-Do bar	
	Notice that the appointment appears on the To-Do Bar and the date corresponding to the day after tomorrow appears in bold in the Date Navigator, indicating that an appointment is scheduled on that day.
9 Click as shown	
	The day after tomorrow appears in the Day view and displays your newly created appointment.
10 Activate Mail	You'll create a message that your partner will use to create an appointment.
Create a new message with the subject **Appointment message**	
Address and send the message to your partner	
11 Check for new messages	Keep checking for new messages until you receive the Appointment message from your partner.

12	Activate Folder List view	(In the Navigation pane, click the Folder List icon.) You'll create an appointment from the Appointment message you received from your partner.
	Drag the Appointment message from your Inbox to the Calendar folder	An Appointment window appears. Notice the message header is inserted into the message body.
	Specify a location	Specify any location, such as "Conference Room."
	Select tomorrow's date in the Start and End date lists	
	Select **9:00 AM** from the Start time list and **10:00 AM** from the End time list	
	Click **Save & Close**	To save the appointment. Notice the appointment is now listed in your To-Do bar.
13	Activate Tasks	You'll create a task request that your partner will use to create an appointment.
	Create a new task request with the subject **Appointment task**	
	Address and send the task request to your partner	In the Manage Task group on the Ribbon, click Assign Task. Address the task request to your partner and click Send.
14	Check for new messages	Keep checking for new messages until you receive the Appointment task from your partner.
15	Activate Folder List view	In the Navigation pane, click the Folder List icon.
16	Drag the Appointment task from your Inbox to the Calendar folder	An Appointment window appears. Notice the task information is inserted into the message body.
	Specify a location	
17	Select tomorrow's date in the Start and End date lists	
	Select **2:00 PM** from the Start time list and **3:00 PM** from the End time list	
	Click **Save & Close**	To save the appointment. Notice the appointment is now listed in your To-Do bar.

repeat

Adding recurring appointments

Explanation

Appointments that occur regularly are known as *recurring appointments*. For example, a quarterly meeting with your regional manager is a recurring appointment. You can schedule recurring appointments by adding the appointments to the Calendar.

 If you want to add a recurring appointment, choose Actions, New Recurring Appointment. This opens a new Appointment window and the Appointment Recurrence dialog box, as shown in Exhibit 6-4. In this dialog box, you specify the start time, the recurrence pattern, and the duration of the appointment. The default Recurrence pattern is Weekly; however, you can also select Daily, Monthly, or Yearly. Each pattern has a different set of options. Under Range of recurrence, you can specify when the recurring appointment will end. Click OK to close the Appointment Recurrence dialog box. Enter the appointment details in the Appointment window and save the appointment.

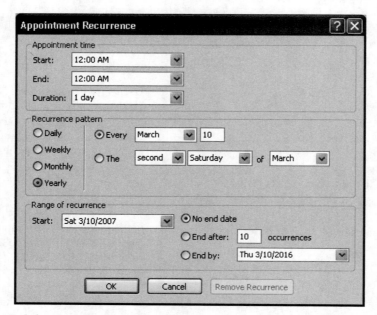

Exhibit 6-4: The Appointment Recurrence dialog box

Do it!   **A-3:   Adding a recurring appointment**

Here's how	Here's why
1 Activate Calendar	
2 Select the current date	(From the Date Navigator.) You'll add a recurring appointment that occurs on the current date.
3 Choose **Actions**, **New Recurring Appointment**	To open the Appointment Recurrence dialog box.
4 Under Appointment time, from the Start list, select **11:00 AM**	To specify the start time of the appointment.
From the Duration list, select **1 hour**	To specify the duration of the appointment. When you specify the duration, the end time is adjusted automatically .
5 Under Recurrence pattern, select **Monthly**	To specify that the appointment takes place every month. The Day box contains the current date, and the "of every <number> month(s)" box contains 1.
6 Click **OK**	To close the Appointment Recurrence dialog box.
Click **OK**	(If necessary.) To close the message box that appears if the current date is the 29th, 30th, or 31st of the month. The message box informs you that some months have fewer than 29, 30, or 31 days and that for these months, the meeting will fall on the last day of the month.
Observe the Recurrence information beneath Location	(In the Untitled – Appointment window.) It displays the recurrence settings for the new appointment. You can modify these settings by clicking the Recurrence button on the Ribbon.
7 Specify the subject as **Monthly appointment with Ann**	In the Subject box.
Specify the location as **Conference Room**	In the Location box.
From the Reminder list, select **None**	To specify that you don't want to be reminded about the appointment.
8 Save the appointment	(Click Save and Close.) The recurrence icon appears to the right of the appointment in the To-Do bar.

Inserting appointments into a message

Explanation

After creating an appointment, you might want to inform others about it. In such cases, you can insert the appointment into an e-mail message as an attachment. To do so:

1 Open a new Message window.

2 Click Attach Item to open the Insert Item dialog box.

3 From the Look in list, select Calendar.

4 From the Items list, select the appointment you want to insert into the message.

5 Click OK to insert the appointment.

Do it!

A-4: Inserting an appointment into a message

Here's how	Here's why
1 Activate Mail	
2 Open a new Message window	
Address the message to your partner	
Specify the subject as **\<yy\>: Meeting Schedule**	
In the Message area, enter **For your information.**	
3 Click **Attach Item**	To open the Insert Item dialog box.
4 From the Look in list, select **Calendar**	You'll insert an appointment from the Calendar.
From the Items list, select **Appointment with Jack**	The appointments are categorized by recurrence status.
Click **OK**	To close the Insert Item dialog box. The selected appointment appears as an attachment in the message.
5 Send the message	
6 Check for new messages	A new message with an attachment from your partner appears in your Inbox folder.

Topic B: Modifying appointments

Explanation   After you create an appointment, you might need to reschedule or cancel it. You can reschedule an appointment by modifying the date, time, location, or other details. You can cancel an appointment by deleting it. You can also restore a deleted appointment.

Editing appointments

Sometimes, you might want to reschedule an appointment to another day or location. To edit an appointment:

1   Double-click the appointment to open it.

2   Make the necessary changes.

3   Click Save & Close.

Do it!   **B-1: Editing an appointment's text**

Here's how	Here's why
1 Display the calendar in a detailed Month view	(Click Month and select the Details High option.) The appointment with Jack has been moved to another location. You'll edit the appointment to reflect this change.
2 Double-click the appointment with the subject Appointment with Jack	(Double-click the appointment in the calendar grid or on the To-Do bar.) To open the Appointment window.
3 Change the start date and the end date to one day later	To postpone the appointment by one day.
Edit the Location box to read **Sales department meeting room**	
4 In the text area, type as shown	1. Arizona Business 2. New Kiosk at Hudson
5 Save the appointment	The appointment is postponed by one day.

Reschedule recurring appointments

If you want to modify a recurring appointment, here's how:

1 Double-click the appointment to open the Open Recurring Item dialog box.

2 If you want to modify a single occurrence, select Open this occurrence. If you want to modify all occurrences of the recurring appointment, select Open the series.

3 Click OK to open the Appointment window.

4 Click Recurrence in the Options group on the Ribbon.

5 Make the necessary changes and click OK.

6 Click Save & Close.

B-2: Modifying a recurring appointment

Here's how	Here's why
1 Open the appointment with the subject Monthly appointment with Ann	(Double-click the appointment.) The Open Recurring Item dialog box appears. You can modify either the selected occurrence or all occurrences of the recurring appointment.
2 Select **Open the series**	You'll change all occurrences of this recurring appointment.
Click **OK**	(To close the Open Recurring Item dialog box.) The Appointment window appears.
3 Click **Recurrence**	(In the Options group on the Ribbon.) To open the Appointment Recurrence dialog box.
Under Appointment time, from the Start list, select **11:30 AM**	
Change the appointment to occur on the last Monday of every month, as shown	The last ▼ Monday ▼ of every 1 month(s)
Close the Appointment Recurrence dialog box	Click OK.
4 Save and close the appointment	The appointment has moved to the last Monday of the month.

Deleting and restoring appointments

Explanation   You can delete appointments that are no longer needed or that have been canceled. To delete an appointment, select it and click the Delete button on the Standard toolbar. You can also press Ctrl+D or choose Edit, Delete.

If a deleted appointment is rescheduled, you can restore it. To restore a deleted appointment, drag it from the Deleted Items folder to the Calendar folder.

Do it!   ### B-3:   Deleting and restoring an appointment

Here's how	Here's why
1 Click as shown	Dec 1 / Appointment
	(Click at the top of the day scheduled for the Appointment with Jack.) The calendar switches to Day view.
2 Select the appointment with the subject Appointment with Jack	(Click the appointment in the calendar grid.) You'll delete this appointment.
3 Click ✗	(On the Standard toolbar.) The appointment is deleted.
4 Open the Deleted Items folder	At the bottom of the Navigation pane, click the Folder List button to activate the Folder list, and click Deleted Items.
5 Drag the appointment with the subject Appointment with Jack to the Calendar folder	(In the Folder List.) To restore the appointment.
6 Activate the Calendar	
Verify that the appointment has been restored	Switch to Month view. The appointment appears in the Calendar view and in the To-Do Bar.

Topic C: Calendar views

This topic covers the following Microsoft Certified Application Specialist exam objectives for Outlook 2007.

#	Objective
2.4.1	Define your work week
2.4.2	Display multiple time zones
2.4.3	Change time zones

Views

Explanation

Outlook provides three Calendar views: Day view, Week view, or Month view. To change the Calendar view, click the appropriate button at the top of the Calendar view. You can view as much of your schedule as you want at a time.

Day view

The default view is Day view, as shown in Exhibit 6-5. This view shows all of your appointments or events for a single day. The current date is selected by default. If you want to view appointments or events for another day, click the forward and back navigation buttons to the left of the date or use the Date Navigator in the To-Do bar.

Exhibit 6-5: Day view

Week view

The default Week view displays all of your appointments and events as a five-day work week, as shown in Exhibit 6-6. If you prefer to view a full seven-day week, select the Show full week option at the top of the Calendar view. If you want to view your appointments for another week, select a day in that week in the Date Navigator.

If your work week is not the typical Monday through Friday, then you can customize the days shown when you display your work week. To customize the days included in the work week view:

1 Choose Tools, Options to open the Options dialog box.
2 Click Calendar Options to open the Calendar Options dialog box.
3 Under Calendar work week, check or clear the check boxes to specify which days should be included in your work week.
4 Click OK twice.

Exhibit 6-6: Week view

The Daily Task list displays under the Calendar view when either Day view or Week view is selected. This list displays your tasks for each day in the selected view.

Do it!   **C-1:   Exploring Day and Week views**

Here's how	Here's why
1 Observe the Calendar view	It displays the appointments for the day.
Click **Day**	(At the top of the Calendar view.) The calendar grid displays the current day. Use this view to see more details of appointments in a single day.
Click as shown	
	To display the calendar for tomorrow.
Click the current date on the Date Navigator	To display the calendar for today.
2 Click **Week**	(At the top of the Calendar view) The calendar grid displays the current work week, Monday to Friday. Use this view to see the appointments and events in the entire work week at a glance.
Select **Show full week**	Notice that the calendar grid now displays the current seven-day week.
Select **Show work week**	To display the work week. You only work Monday through Thursday, so you'll customize the work week view to include only those days.
3 Choose **Tools**, **Options...**	To open the Options dialog box.
4 Click **Calendar Options**	To open the Calendar Options dialog box.
Under Calendar work week, clear **Fri**	
Click **OK**	To return to the Options dialog box.
5 Click **OK**	The work week view now includes only Monday through Thursday. You'll change the view to again to include Friday.
6 Open the Calendar Options dialog box	Choose Tools, Options to open the Options dialog box. Click Calendar Options.
Under Calendar work week, check **Fri**	
Click **OK**	To return to the Options dialog box.
7 Click **OK**	The work week view again includes Monday through Friday.
8 Click **Day**	To switch back to the default view.

Month view

Explanation

You can also view your scheduled appointments and events for an entire month. By default, Month view displays only your events and the Daily Task list isn't displayed, as shown in Exhibit 6-7.

You can change the amount of detail that you want displayed in the calendar grid by selecting one of the Details options—Low, Medium, or High—at the top of the Calendar view. The Low option is the default view. Low view displays only events in the calendar grid. The Medium option displays events and appointments as a solid bar in the calendar grid cell. The High option displays events and appointments, as well as the start times, subject, and location for each appointment.

Exhibit 6-7: A sample Month view in high detail

Do it!   ## C-2: Exploring Month view

Here's how	Here's why
1 Click **Month**	To display the planner for the entire month.
Observe the calendar grid	It shows the current month.
Click as shown	

To display next month.

| 2 Select **Medium** | |

(Next to Details at the top of the Calendar view.) Notice that the date containing the recurring appointment now has a blue bar indicating the appointment.

| 3 Select **High** | |

(Next to Details at the top of the Calendar view.) Notice that the date containing the recurring appointment now shows the details of the appointment.

Point to the recurring appointment

The ScreenTip shows the appointment details.

Setting workdays and times

Explanation

The default work week is Monday through Friday, and the workday begins at 8:00 A.M. and ends at 5:00 P.M. You might want to change the workdays or the times of the day. You can change these calendar options by using the Calendar Options dialog box, shown in Exhibit 6-8.

To change the workday and times:

1 Choose Tools, Options to open the Options dialog box.

2 Under Calendar, click Calendar Options to open the Calendar Options dialog box.

3 Under Calendar work week, check or clear the days to indicate your work week.

4 In the Start time box, select the time when your workday begins.

5 In the End time box, select the time when your workday ends.

6 Click OK twice to save changes and close all the dialog boxes.

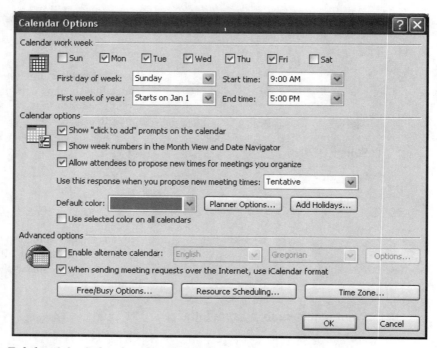

Exhibit 6-8: Calendar Options dialog box

Do it!

C-3: Changing the workday times

Here's how	Here's why
1 Choose **Tools**, **Options...**	To open the Options dialog box.
Verify that the Preferences tab is activated	
2 Under Calendar, click **Calendar Options**	To open the Calendar Options dialog box.
3 Under Calendar work week, change the Start time to **9:00 AM**	To change the work week start time.
4 Click **OK**	To close the Calendar Options dialog box.
5 Click **OK**	To close the Option dialog box.
6 Activate Calendar	If necessary.
Switch to Day view	Notice that the day now automatically opens to the 9:00 AM time slot.

Setting up multiple time zones

Explanation

You might have business associates or clients who are located around the world. When scheduling activities such as conference calls, you need to consider the time zones for these locations. You can add time zones to help you schedule your activities.

To create a new time zone:

1 Choose Tools, Options to open the Options dialog box.
2 Under Calendar, click Calendar Options to open the Calendar Options dialog box.
3 Under Advanced options, click Time Zone to open the Time Zone dialog box.
4 Check Show an additional time zone.
5 In the Label box, enter the label you want to display before the new time zone.
6 From the Time zone list, select the time zone you want to add.
7 If you want to adjust for daylight saving time, check the Adjust for daylight saving time option.
8 Click OK three times to save changes and close all the dialog boxes.

Do it!

C-4: Displaying multiple time zones

Here's how	Here's why
1 Choose **Tools, Options...**	To open the Options dialog box.
Verify that the Preferences tab is activated	
2 Under Calendar, click **Calendar Options**	To open the Calendar Options dialog box.
3 Under Advanced options, click **Time Zone**	To open the Time Zone dialog box.
Observe the Current time zone settings	The settings display your local time zone and the daylight saving time setting.
In the Label box, enter **HQ**	You'll use the label HQ to identify your local time zone.

4 Check **Show an additional time zone**

To specify another time zone. The options under this group are now available.

Under Show an additional time zone, in the Label box, enter **GMT**

To specify the text you want to display to identify the additional time zone.

From the Time zone list, select as shown

(GMT-06:00) Central Time (US & Canada)
(GMT-05:00) Indiana (East)
(GMT-04:00) Atlantic Time (Canada)
(GMT-04:00) Caracas, La Paz
(GMT-04:00) Santiago
(GMT-03:30) Newfoundland
(GMT-03:00) Brasilia
(GMT-03:00) Buenos Aires, Georgetown
(GMT-03:00) Greenland
(GMT-02:00) Mid-Atlantic
(GMT-01:00) Azores
(GMT-01:00) Cape Verde Is.
(GMT) Casablanca, Monrovia
(GMT) Greenwich Mean Time : Dublin, Edinburgh, Lisbo
(GMT+01:00) Amsterdam, Berlin, Bern, Rome, Stockho
(GMT+01:00) Belgrade, Bratislava, Budapest, Ljubljana
(GMT+01:00) Brussels, Copenhagen, Madrid, Paris

(The GMT time zone.) To add a time zone.

5 Click **OK**

To close the Time Zone dialog box.

6 Click **OK**

To apply the changes and close the Calendar Options dialog box.

7 Click **OK**

To close the Options dialog box.

8 Switch to Day view

GMT	HQ
2 pm	9 am
3 00	10 00
4 00	11 00
5 00	12 pm
6 00	1 00

(If necessary.) The time zones are not visible in Month view. The time zones with the labels GMT and HQ appear to the left of the calendar grid.

Specifying a new time zone

Explanation

If you move or travel to a different time zone, you can change the time zone for the Calendar to update all items to reflect the new time zone. For example, if you travel to a time zone that is one hour later than your specified time zone, then you can switch the Calendar to the new time zone so that all Calendar items update by one hour. A meeting scheduled for 10 AM in your old time zone will now appear as being scheduled for 11 AM.

To change your time zone:

1 Open the Calendar Options dialog box.
2 Click Time Zone to open the Time Zone dialog box.
3 Under Current Windows time zone, from the Time zone list, select the new time zone.
4 Click OK to close each dialog box.

Do it!

C-5: Changing your time zone

Here's how	Here's why
1 Open the Calendar Options dialog box	Choose Tools, Options. Click Calendar Options.
2 Click **Time Zone**	To open the Time Zone dialog box.
3 Under Additional time zone, from the Time zone list, select a different time zone	Be sure to select a time zone that is one or two hours different from your original time zone.
4 Click **OK**	To return to the Calendar Options dialog box.
5 Click **OK**	To return to the Options dialog box.
6 Click **OK**	Your scheduled items' times are automatically updated to reflect the new time zone.
7 Return to your original time zone	

Topic D: Events

This topic covers the following Microsoft Certified Application Specialist exam objectives for Outlook 2007.

#	Objective
2.1.1	Create a one-time appointment, meeting, or event
2.1.2	Create a recurring appointment, meeting, or event
2.1.3	Create an appointment, meeting, or event from an e-mail message
2.1.4	Create an appointment, meeting, or event from a task
2.1.5	Mark an appointment, meeting, or event as private
2.4.4	Add pre-defined holidays to the Calendar

Creating events

Explanation

In Outlook, an *event* is an activity that lasts for a period of one or more days and that can be added to the Calendar. There are three types of events in Outlook: single-day, multi-day, and annual. For example, workshops, conferences, and seminars can be single or multi-day events, whereas birthdays and anniversaries are annual events that occur on fixed dates. By default, Outlook assumes that events last for at least one day. However, you can change this setting and specify the duration of an event.

Single and multi-day events

Single-day events are events that last for a single day. *Multi-day events* are events that last for one or more days. You can add single and multi-day events to the Calendar. Here's how:

1 Choose Actions, New All Day Event to open a new Event window.
2 Specify the subject and location for the event.
3 Do one of the following:
   - If it is a single-day event that runs for the entire day, select the same date for the start and end dates. Notice that All day event is checked by default.
   - If it is a multi-day event, select the dates for the start and end dates.
4 From the Reminder list on the Ribbon, select when you want to be reminded about the event.
5 Click Save and Close to save the event and close the Event window.

Creating events from messages and tasks

You can also create events from messages and tasks. To do so, click the Folder List icon in the Navigation pane. Then, drag the event to the Calendar folder or Tasks folder. When the Event window appears, configure and save the event.

Marking an event as private

You can mark an event as private to prevent other people from accessing the details of your personal events. Use the private designation only when you share folders with people whom you trust. To mark an event as private, open the event and click Private in the Options group.

Do it!

D-1: Adding a multi-day event

Here's how	Here's why
1 Display the calendar in Month view	
2 Choose **Actions**, **New All Day Event**	To open a new Event window.
3 In the Subject box, enter **Medicinal spice seminar**	
4 Specify the start date as the first Monday of the next month	Use the Date Navigator to advance to the next month.
5 Specify the end date as the date that is three working days from the start date	
Observe the Reminder list	Notice that the default reminder is set for 18 hours before the event.
Click **Private**	(In the Options group on the Ribbon.) To mark the event as a private event.
6 Click **Save & Close**	To save the event and close the Event window.
7 View the first Monday of next month	(Advance to the next month, and view the first Monday.) The event appears as a banner across the scheduled days.
8 Explore other Calendar views	To examine how the event appears in the other views.
9 Activate Mail	You'll create a message that your partner will use to create an event.
10 Create a new message with the subject **Event message**	
Address and send the message to your partner	

11	Check for new messages	Keep checking for new messages until you receive the Event message from your partner.
12	Activate Folder List view	(In the Navigation pane, click the Folder List icon.) You'll create an event from the Event message you received from your partner.
13	Drag the Appointment message from your Inbox to the Calendar folder	An Event window appears. Notice that the message header is inserted into the message body.
	Specify a location	
14	Select tomorrow's date in the Start and End date lists	
	Verify that All day event is checked	Notice if you clear this box, the event turns into an appointment.
	Click **Save & Close**	To save the event. Notice the event is now listed in your To-Do bar.
15	Activate Tasks	You'll create a task request that your partner will use to create an event.
	Create a new task request with the subject **Event task**	
	Address and send the message to your partner	
16	Check for new messages	Keep checking for new messages until you receive the Event task from your partner.
17	Activate Folder List view	In the Navigation pane, click the Folder List icon.
18	Drag the Event task from your Inbox to the Calendar folder	An Event window appears. Notice the task information is inserted into the message body.
	Specify a location	
	In the Start and End date lists, select a date other than tomorrow	
	Check **All day event**	
	Click **Save & Close**	To save the event.
19	Activate Calendar	
20	Switch to Day view	
	Locate the Event task date	The event appears as a banner across the scheduled day.

Add annual events

Explanation

An *annual event* is an event that occurs every year on a specific day. You can add an annual event, such as a birthday, to your Calendar. To do so:

1   Choose Actions, New All Day Event to open the new Event window.
2   Enter the details of the event such as subject, location, and date.
3   Click Recurrence to open the Appointment Recurrence dialog box.
4   Under Recurrence pattern, select Yearly.
5   Click OK.
6   Click Save & Close.

Do it!   **D-2: Adding an annual event**

Here's how	Here's why
1 Open a new Event window	Choose Actions, New All Day Event.
Specify the subject as **Annual day**	(In the Subject box.) To create a new event with the subject "Annual day."
2 From the Start time list, select **March 10**	To specify the date of the annual event. Depending on the current date, you might notice a message in the InfoBar, which tells you that the selected date occurs in the past. Because this event will be changed to an annual one, you can ignore this message.
3 Open the Appointment Recurrence dialog box	Click Recurrence.
Under Recurrence pattern, select **Yearly**	
Verify that the recurrence period is selected as shown	⊙ Every March ▾ 10
4 Close the Appointment Recurrence dialog box	Click OK.
5 Save the event	
6 Select **March 10**	10 Saturday Annual day ↻
	(Using the Date Navigator in the To-Do bar.) The event appears as a banner at the top of the Day view.
7 Display the Calendar for next year	Click the right arrow on the Date Navigator.
Select **March 10**	The event appears as a banner at the top of the Day view.
8 Click **Today**	(The Today button is on the Standard toolbar.) To display the current date in the Calendar view.

Holidays

Explanation

You can display holidays commonly celebrated in your country in the Calendar. Holidays appear on the Calendar as all-day events.

To add the holidays to the Calendar:

1 Open the Calendar Options dialog box.

2 Under Calendar options, click Add Holidays to open the Add Holidays to Calendar dialog box.

3 In the list of countries, check your country.

4 Click OK. A message indicates that the holidays are added to your Calendar.

5 Click OK to return to the Calendar Options dialog box.

6 Click OK twice to close the remaining dialog boxes.

Do it!   **D-3:   Adding holidays to the calendar**

Here's how	Here's why
1 Open the Calendar Options dialog box	
2 Under Calendar options, click **Add Holidays**	To open the Add Holidays to Calendar dialog box.
3 Verify that your country is checked	
4 Click **OK**	To import the holidays to your Calendar. A message indicates that the holidays have been added.
Click **OK**	To return to the Calendar Options dialog box.
5 Click **OK** twice	To close the remaining dialog boxes. The holidays commonly celebrated in your country now appear on your Calendar as all-day events.

Unit summary: Appointments and events

Topic A   In this topic, you learned about the Calendar interface, including the **Calendar pane**, the **Calendar view**, the **To-Do bar**, and the **Daily Task list**. You used the Calendar to **set up** an appointment by using the Appointment window or by using the Click to Add Appointment feature. You also learned how to add a **recurring appointment**. Then, you learned how to make an appointment private and how to add an event from a message or a task. You also learned how to **insert** an appointment into a message.

Topic B   In this topic, you learned how to **edit** an appointment. You also modified a recurring appointment. Then, you **deleted** an appointment that is no longer needed and **restored** a deleted appointment.

Topic C   In this topic, you learned how to display your scheduled appointments by using different views, such as Day, Week, and Month. Then, you **changed** the **workday times** and **added a time zone**.

Topic D   In this topic, you added a **multi-day event** and **annual events** to the Calendar. You also learned how to mark an event as private and how to add an event from a message or a task. Then, you learned how to add holidays to your Calendar.

Independent practice activity

In this activity, you'll create a recurring appointment. You'll view an appointment, and will delete and restore it. In addition, you'll e-mail an appointment. Finally, you'll create an annual event.

1 Set up an appointment with Kim for tomorrow at 9:00 A.M. Specify the subject as **Meeting with Kim**, the location as **Holiday Inn**, and the end time as 10:30 A.M.

2 Make the appointment a recurring appointment, repeating every month for four months. (*Hint:* Under Range of recurrence, specify the relevant value in the End after box.)

3 Save the appointment.

4 Observe the appointment Meeting with Kim in the various Calendar views and on the To-Do bar.

5 Delete all occurrences of the appointment Meeting with Kim, and then restore them.

6 Insert the appointment Meeting with Kim into a message, and send it to your partner.

7 Create an event with the subject **Annual Distributors Meeting**.

8 Make this event recur annually on September 10.

9 Save the event.

Review questions

1 Which of the following can be used to display a different month? (Select all that apply.)

   A The forward and back navigation buttons in Month view

   B Current View list

   C Date Navigator

   D Daily Task list

2 What is the difference between an appointment, a meeting, and an event?

3 What is the definition of a recurring appointment?

4 How do you create a recurring appointment?

5 Which Standard toolbar button can you use to quickly display the appointments for the current day?

6 What is the procedure to change your calendar so that every day starts at 9:00 A.M.?

7 What is the main difference between appointments and events?

8 How many days are shown in the default Week view?

9 Which of the following Month view Details options displays a blue bar indicating an appointment?

A Low

B Medium

C High

D Daily Task list

10 If you delete an appointment and then find that you still need it, how do you restore it to the Calendar?

Unit 7

Meeting requests and responses

Unit time: 50 minutes

Complete this unit, and you'll know how to:

A Use the Calendar to plan a meeting; create and send a meeting request; and understand the function of a meeting workspace.

B Read and respond to meeting requests by accepting or declining them or by proposing a new meeting time.

C Review meeting responses, and update and cancel meetings.

Topic A: Meeting requests

This topic covers the following Microsoft Certified Application Specialist exam objectives for Outlook 2007.

#	Objective
2.1.1	Create a one-time appointment, meeting, or event
2.1.2	Create a recurring appointment, meeting, or event
2.1.3	Create an appointment, meeting, or event from an e-mail message
2.1.4	Create an appointment, meeting, or event from a task
2.1.5	Mark an appointment, meeting, or event as private
2.2.1	Invite mandatory attendees to meetings
2.2.2	Invite optional attendees to meetings
2.2.5	Schedule meeting resources
2.3.3	Modify one instance of a recurring meeting

Organizing a meeting

Explanation

You can use the Calendar's *Plan a Meeting* feature to schedule meetings. You can set a time, duration, location, and agenda for your meeting. In addition, you can schedule other resources that you might need, such as a projector, VCR, computer, or flip chart. After scheduling a meeting, you can send a meeting request to all the attendees. A *meeting request* contains all the details of a meeting proposal, such as time, date, and subject. You can also announce a meeting over the Web by using Outlook.

Before creating and sending a meeting request, you can create a plan for the meeting. To do this:

1 Activate the Calendar and choose Actions, Plan a Meeting to open the Plan a Meeting window, shown in Exhibit 7-1. You can also click the Plan a Meeting button on the Advanced toolbar to open the Plan a Meeting window.

2 Click Add Others and choose Add from Address Book to open the Select Attendees and Resources dialog box. Specify the attendees and the resources you'd like to have at the meeting. There are four types of attendees: the meeting organizer, required attendees, optional attendees, and resources. Outlook automatically retrieves the schedule information and availability of the selected attendees.

3 In the Meeting start time and Meeting end time boxes, specify the start and end times. You can alter the meeting time to suit your attendees' schedules.

4 When an acceptable meeting time is found, click Make Meeting to open a new Meeting window. Outlook automatically fills in the attendees, resources, date, and duration of the meeting based on the details you entered in the Plan a Meeting window.

Attendee status   Time planner

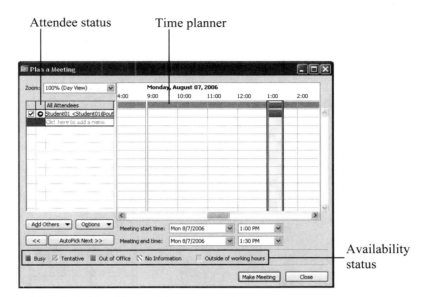

Availability
status

Exhibit 7-1: The Plan a Meeting window

Do it! **A-1: Planning a meeting**

Here's how	Here's why
1 Activate the Calendar	If necessary.
2 Click ▦	(The Plan a Meeting button is on the Advanced toolbar.) To open the Plan a Meeting window.
Observe the All Attendees list	☑ ⚙ Student01
	Because you are the meeting owner, your name appears at the top of the list. Outlook assumes that you're one of the attendees. The icon to the left of your name identifies you as the meeting organizer. This status cannot be changed.
3 Click **Add Others**	Add Others ▾ Options ▾ Add from Address Book... Add Public Folder...
	To display the menu.
Choose **Add from Address Book...**	To open the Select Attendees and Resources dialog box.
4 From the Name list, select your partner's name	You'll invite your partner to the meeting as a required participant.
Click **Required**	To add your partner's name to the list of mandatory attendees.
5 From the Name list, select another student's name	You'll invite another student to the meeting as an optional participant.
Click **Optional**	
6 From the Name list, select **Projector**	You'll add a resource for the meeting.
Click **Resources**	

7 Click **OK**

To close the Select Attendees and Resources dialog box. Your partner's name appears in the All Attendees list.

✉	All Attendees
✓ ⬤	Student01
✓ ⬆	Student02
✓ 🟡	Student03
✓ 🔲	Projector
	Click here to add a name

Observe the icons to the left of each attendee and resource

Each icon identifies the attendee as either the meeting organizer, required attendee, optional attendee, or resource (as shown from top to bottom). As you may have noticed earlier, you're identified as the meeting organizer, and your status cannot be changed. However, you can change the status of other attendees by clicking the icon to display a menu.

8 From the first Meeting start list, select a start date

To specify the start date for the meeting. Notice that the end date is the same as the start date.

If you belong to Group A, select the next Monday as the start date. If you belong to Group B, choose the next Tuesday as the start date.

9 From the second Meeting start list, select **3:00 PM**

To specify the start time of the meeting.

From the second Meeting end time list, select
5:00 PM (2 hours)

To specify the end time of the meeting. The time planner presents the meeting time with a green line representing the start time and a red line representing the end time. You can also tell if an attendee will be busy or out of the office on that date and time so you can select a new date or time.

Creating and sending meeting requests

Explanation

You can also create a meeting request without going through the Plan a Meeting window.

There are several ways to open a new Meeting window:

- Activate the Calendar and then choose Actions, New Meeting Request.
- Choose File, New, Meeting Request.
- Click the New button's down arrow on the Standard toolbar and choose Meeting Request.
- Press Ctrl+Shift+Q.

In the Meeting window, you enter the subject and other details of the meeting. You can check the attendees' availability, resource details, and meeting time availability by clicking the Scheduling button in the Show group on the Ribbon. Click the Send button to send the meeting request to the attendees. After you send the meeting request, the meeting appears as an appointment in your Calendar and on the To-Do bar.

Creating meetings from messages and tasks

You can also create meetings from messages and tasks. To do so, click the Folder List icon in the Navigation pane. Locate and select the message or task. Then, drag the message or task to the Calendar folder. When the Appointment window appears, click Invite Attendees in the Actions group on the Ribbon. The window turns into a Meeting window. Enter the recipients, meeting subject, and location. Click Scheduling to find a time when all recipients are available. Then click Send to send the meeting request.

Marking a meeting as private

You can mark a meeting as private to prevent other people from accessing the details about the meeting. To ensure that other people cannot read the items that you mark as private, do not grant them Read permission to your Calendar, Contacts, or Tasks folders. Use the private designation only when you share folders with people whom you trust. To mark a meeting as private, open the appointment and click Private in the Options group.

Do it!

A-2: Creating and sending a meeting request

Here's how	Here's why
1 Click **Make Meeting**	To open a new Meeting window. The InfoBar specifies that invitations have not been sent for the meeting. Your partner's name appears in the To box.
2 In the Subject box, enter **\<xx\>: Sales strategy for the Midwest region**	To specify the subject. In place of \<xx\>, use your partner's number. Outlook has entered the start and end times that you specified in the Plan a Meeting window.
In the Location box, enter **Conference Room**	To specify the location for the meeting.

3 Observe the Reminder list — (In the Options group on the Ribbon.) It is set to remind you 15 minutes before the meeting.

Select **None**

Verify from the Show as list that Busy is selected — To mark the allocated time as busy in your Calendar. Other options are Free, Tentative, and Out of Office.

4 Click **Private** — (In the Options group on the Ribbon. Depending on the window size, the Private button may or may not display the word "Private.") To make the meeting private.

5 Click **Send** — To send the meeting request.

6 Observe the Plan a Meeting window

The solid blue bar identifies this meeting time as busy for the meeting organizer. The attendees' time will be updated when they respond to the meeting request.

7 Click **Close** — To close the Plan a Meeting window.

8 Activate Mail — You'll create a message that your partner will use to create a meeting.

Create a new message with the subject **Meeting message**

Address and send the message to your partner

9 Check for new messages — Keep checking for new messages until you receive the Meeting message from your partner.

10 Activate Folder List view — (In the Navigation pane, click the Folder List icon.) You'll create a meeting from the Meeting message you received from your partner.

Drag the Meeting message from your Inbox to the Calendar folder — An Appointment window appears. Notice that the message header is inserted into the message body.

Click **Invite Attendees** — (In the Actions group on the Ribbon.) To change the Appointment window to a Meeting window.

11 Address the meeting request to your partner	
Specify a location	
Select tomorrow's date in the Start and End date lists	
Select **9:00 AM** from the Start time list and **10:00 AM** from the End time list	
Click **Send**	To send the meeting request. Notice the meeting is now listed in your To-Do bar.
12 Activate Tasks	You'll create a task request that your partner will use to create a meeting.
Create a new task request with the subject **Meeting task**	
Address and send the message to your partner	
13 Check for new messages	Keep checking for new messages until you receive the Meeting task from your partner.
14 Activate Folder List view	In the Navigation pane, click the Folder List icon.
Drag the Meeting task from your Inbox to the Calendar folder	
Click **Invite Attendees**	
15 Address the meeting request to your partner	
Specify a location	A Meeting window appears. Notice the task information is inserted into the message body.
Select tomorrow's date in the Start and End date lists	
Select **2:00 PM** from the Start time list and **3:00 PM** from the End time list	
Click **Send**	To send the meeting request. Notice the meeting is now listed in your To-Do bar.

Recurring meetings

Explanation

Meetings that occur regularly are known as *recurring meetings*. For example, a quarterly sales meeting is a recurring meeting. You can schedule recurring meetings by adding the meeting to the Calendar.

If you want to add a recurring meeting, choose Actions, New Recurring Meeting. This opens a new Appointment window and the Appointment Recurrence dialog box, as shown in Exhibit 7-2. In this dialog box, you specify the start time, the recurrence pattern, and the duration of the appointment. The default Recurrence pattern is Weekly; however, you can also select Daily, Monthly, or Yearly. Each pattern has a different set of options. Under Range of recurrence, you can specify when the recurring meeting will end. Click OK to close the Appointment Recurrence dialog box. Enter the meeting details in the Meeting window, and then save the meeting.

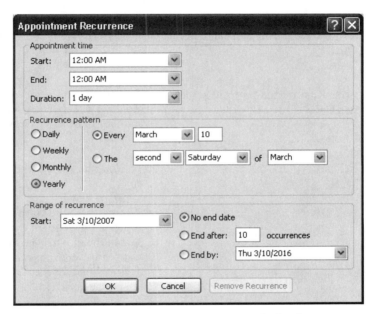

Exhibit 7-2: The Appointment Recurrence dialog box

A-3:   Adding a recurring meeting

Here's how	Here's why
1 Activate Calendar	
2 Select the current date	(From the Date Navigator.) You'll add a recurring meeting that occurs on the current date.
3 Choose **Actions**, **New Recurring Meeting**	To open the Appointment Recurrence dialog box.
4 Under Appointment time, from the Start list, select **1:00 PM**	To specify the start time of the meeting .
From the Duration list, select **1 hour**	To specify the duration of the meeting. When you specify the duration, the end time is adjusted automatically.
5 Under Recurrence pattern, select **Monthly**	To specify that the meeting takes place every month. The Day box contains the current date, and the "of every <number> month(s)" box contains 1.
6 Click **OK**	To close the Appointment Recurrence dialog box.
Click **OK**	(If necessary.) To close the message box that appears if the current date is the 29th, 30th, or 31st of the month. The message box informs you that some months have fewer than 29, 30, or 31 days and that for these months, the meeting will fall on the last day of the month.
Observe the Recurrence information beneath Location	(In the Untitled – Appointment window.) It displays the recurrence settings for the new meeting. You can modify these settings by clicking the Recurrence button on the Ribbon.
7 Click **To**	To open the Select Attendees and Resources dialog box.
8 In the Name list, select your partner	You'll make your partner a required attendee.
Click **Required**	
9 In the Name list, select another student, press (CTRL), and select a second student	You'll make these students optional attendees.
Click **Optional**	
Click **OK**	

10	Specify the subject as **Monthly marketing meeting**	(In the Subject box.) Every month you have a marketing meeting. So, instead of creating the meeting every month, you'll create a recurring meeting.
	Specify the location as **Conference Room**	In the Location box.
	From the Reminder list, select **None**	To specify that you don't want to be reminded about the meeting.
11	Send the meeting request	The recurrence icon appears to the right of the meeting in the To-Do bar.

Modifying a recurring meeting

Explanation

When you modify a recurring meeting, you can either modify the entire series or a single occurrence of the meeting. Open the meeting and then select either Open this occurrence or Open the series. Make your changes and click Send Update to send an update to your meeting attendees.

Do it!

A-4: Modifying a recurring meeting

Here's how	Here's why
1 Activate Calendar	You'll change the time for the next occurrence of the Monthly marketing meeting
2 Double-click the next occurrence of the Monthly marketing meeting	
Verify Open this occurrence is selected	You want to modify only a single occurrence of the meeting.
Click **OK**	
3 Change the start time to **2:00 PM**	
4 Click **Send Update**	To send an update to the attendees.

Topic B: Meeting request responses

This topic covers the following Microsoft Certified Application Specialist exam objective for Outlook 2007.

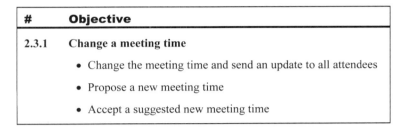

#	Objective
2.3.1	**Change a meeting time**
	• Change the meeting time and send an update to all attendees
	• Propose a new meeting time
	• Accept a suggested new meeting time

Read and accept a meeting request

Explanation

You can read a meeting request to determine the meeting's date, time, location, duration, subject, and attendees. To read a meeting request, double-click the meeting request message in your Inbox. The meeting request opens in a Meeting window, as shown in Exhibit 7-3. You can also read the details of the meeting request in the Reading Pane by selecting the meeting request message.

Depending on your availability, you'll tell the meeting organizer whether you can attend the meeting. To reply to a meeting request, click the relevant button on the Ribbon. If you click Accept, Tentative, or Propose New Time, Outlook enters the meeting as an appointment in your Calendar and on your To-Do bar. To accept a meeting request, open it and click the Accept button in the Respond group on the Ribbon.

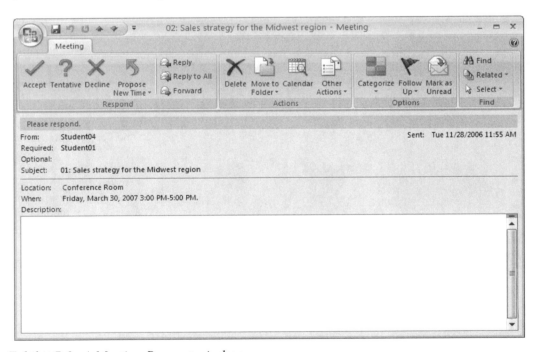

Exhibit 7-3: A Meeting Request window

Do it!

B-1:   Reading and accepting a meeting request

Here's how	Here's why
1 Activate Mail	
Check for new messages	
Observe the new message	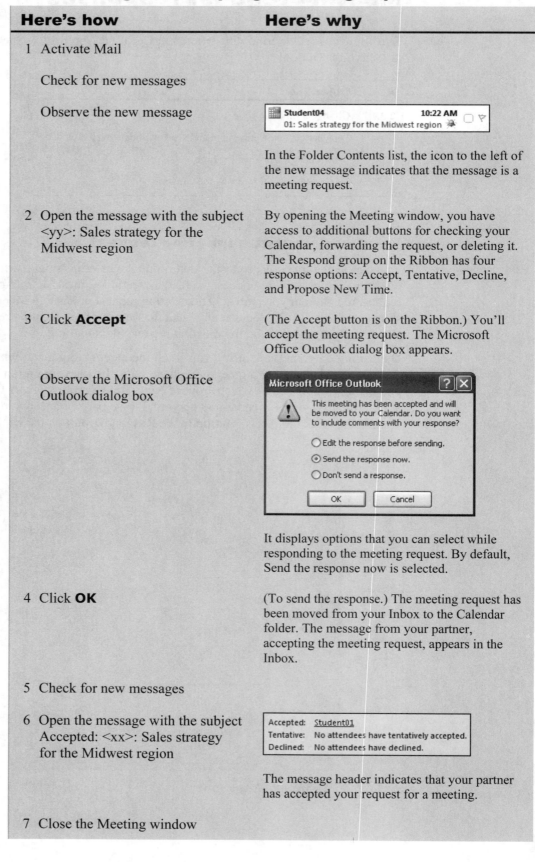
	In the Folder Contents list, the icon to the left of the new message indicates that the message is a meeting request.
2 Open the message with the subject <yy>: Sales strategy for the Midwest region	By opening the Meeting window, you have access to additional buttons for checking your Calendar, forwarding the request, or deleting it. The Respond group on the Ribbon has four response options: Accept, Tentative, Decline, and Propose New Time.
3 Click **Accept**	(The Accept button is on the Ribbon.) You'll accept the meeting request. The Microsoft Office Outlook dialog box appears.
Observe the Microsoft Office Outlook dialog box	
	It displays options that you can select while responding to the meeting request. By default, Send the response now is selected.
4 Click **OK**	(To send the response.) The meeting request has been moved from your Inbox to the Calendar folder. The message from your partner, accepting the meeting request, appears in the Inbox.
5 Check for new messages	
6 Open the message with the subject Accepted: <xx>: Sales strategy for the Midwest region	
	The message header indicates that your partner has accepted your request for a meeting.
7 Close the Meeting window	

Propose a new time for meetings

Explanation

If a meeting time does not fit your schedule, you can suggest an alternative time instead of declining the meeting. However, the meeting organizer controls whether or not attendees can propose a new time.

To propose a new time for the meeting:

1 Open the meeting request message.

2 Click Propose New Time and select either Tentative and Propose New Time or Decline and Propose New Time to open the Propose New Time dialog box. Here, you can modify the date and time, but you can't change the attendee list.

3 Modify the date and time.

4 Click Propose Time to open a new Meeting Response window, as shown in Exhibit 7-4.

5 Click Send. As the meeting organizer, you'll receive a New Time Proposed message in your Inbox.

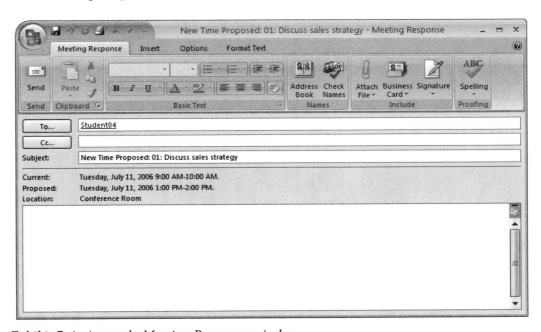

Exhibit 7-4: A sample Meeting Response window

Do it!

B-2: Receiving a New Time Proposed message

Here's how	Here's why
1 Activate the Calendar	
2 Choose **Actions**, **New Meeting Request**	To open a new Meeting window. You'll create a new meeting request.
In the To box, enter the name of your partner	You'll send the meeting request to your partner.
	If the InfoBar displays a message indicating a conflict, you can ignore this message because you'll be proposing a new time for this meeting.
In the Subject box, enter **<xx>: Discuss sales strategy**	
In the Location box, enter **Conference Room**	
3 Specify the start date as the day after tomorrow	From the first Start time list, select the day after tomorrow.
Specify the start time	If you belong to Group A, specify 11:00 A.M. If you belong to Group B, specify 1:00 P.M. If you are not in a group, specify 3:00 P.M.
Verify that the end date is the same as the start date	
Specify the end time	If you belong to Group A, specify 1:00 P.M. If you belong to Group B, specify 3:00 P.M. If you are not in a group, specify 5:00 P.M.
4 Click **Send**	To send the meeting request to your partner.
5 Activate Mail	
Check for new messages	The content of the meeting request sent by your partner appears in the Reading pane.
6 Open the message with the subject <yy>: Discuss sales strategy	This is the meeting request sent to you by your partner.
Click **Propose New Time**	
Select **Tentative and Propose New Time**	To open the Propose New Time: Discuss sales strategy dialog box.
Observe the time planner	The time slot for you appears as tentative because you haven't accepted the meeting request yet.

7 Click **AutoPick Next**	To select the next available time slot for all attendees and resources.
8 Click **Propose Time**	To open a new Meeting Response window. The Meeting Response window indicates that you're proposing a new time. It also displays the meeting's original time and the new time proposed.
Send the meeting request	(Click Send.) To send your proposed new meeting time to your partner.
9 Check for new messages	
10 Open the message with the subject New Time Proposed: <xx>: Discuss sales strategy	It displays the time proposed by your partner for the meeting organized by you. You'll accept your partner's proposed new meeting time.
Click **Accept Proposal**	To accept the meeting time suggested by your partner and reschedule the meeting. The Meeting window appears.
Click **Send Update**	To send an update message to the attendees and close the Meeting window.
11 Check for new messages	
12 Open the message with the subject <yy>: Discuss sales strategy	
13 Click **Accept**	(The Microsoft Office Outlook dialog box appears.) You'll accept the request to attend the meeting at the time you proposed.
Click **OK**	To close the dialog box and send the response.
Check for new messages	A message from your partner, accepting the meeting request, appears in the Folder Contents list.
14 Activate the Calendar	The meeting appears as an appointment in the Calendar. If you don't see the appointment, select the date from the Date Navigator.

Decline meeting requests

Explanation

Before responding to a meeting request, you can check your schedule by clicking the Calendar button in the Meeting window. The Calendar opens and displays the proposed meeting as an appointment. If you have another appointment that conflicts with the meeting request, a message indicating this conflict appears on the InfoBar.

When you receive a conflicting meeting request, you can decline the request. You do this by clicking the Decline button in the Message window or in the Reading pane.

When you decline a meeting request, the organizer receives a message saying that you have declined the meeting request. Declined meeting requests will not be added to your Calendar.

Do it!

B-3: Declining a meeting request

Here's how	Here's why
1 Open a new Meeting window	Activate Calendar, if necessary, and choose Actions, New Meeting Request.
Address the meeting request to your partner	In the To box, enter the name of your partner.
Specify the subject as **<xx>: Quarterly sales review**	
Specify the Location as **Conference Room**	
2 Specify the start date as the day after tomorrow	
Specify a start time	If you belong to Group A, specify 11:00 A.M. If you belong to Group B, specify 1:00 P.M. If you are not in a group, specify 3:00 P.M.
Specify the end time	If you belong to Group A, specify 1:00 P.M. If you belong to Group B, specify 3:00 P.M. If you are not in a group, specify 5:00 P.M.
3 Send the meeting request	
4 Activate Mail	
Check for new messages	

5 Select the message with the subject <yy>: Quarterly sales review	(If necessary.) The contents of the meeting request appear in the Reading pane.
Click **Decline**	(The Decline button is in the Reading pane.) To decline the meeting request from your partner. You'll decline this meeting request because you have meetings scheduled for the day after tomorrow and you can't propose a new time because you're too busy. Also, this meeting request conflicts with another appointment. The Microsoft Office Outlook dialog box appears.
Observe the Microsoft Office Outlook dialog box	By default, Edit the response before sending is selected. Use this option to add a comment to explain why you're declining the meeting.
6 Select **Send the response now**	
Click **OK**	To close the Microsoft Office Outlook dialog box.
7 Activate Mail	If necessary.
Check for new messages	
8 Observe the message with the subject Declined: <xx>: Quarterly sales review	Student01 Declined: Quarterly sales review The message indicates that your partner has declined the meeting request. Because you're the meeting organizer, the meeting is still in your Calendar. If you don't want to have the meeting, you'll have to delete it from your Calendar.

Topic C: Managing meeting responses

This topic covers the following Microsoft Certified Application Specialist exam objectives for Outlook 2007.

#	Objective
2.2.4	Track responses to meeting requests
2.3.1	Change a meeting time
	• Change the meeting time and send an update to all attendees
	• Propose a new meeting time
	• Accept a suggested new meeting time
2.3.2	Add a meeting attendee
2.3.4	Send meeting updates only to new attendees
2.3.5	Cancel a meeting

Viewing meeting responses

Explanation

You need to know how the attendees of a meeting have responded so that you can decide whether to reschedule the meeting or change its venue. For example, if most of the attendees are not available at the proposed time, you can reschedule the meeting. You might even have to cancel a meeting.

To review the responses of the attendees, open the Meeting window and click the Tracking button, as shown in Exhibit 7-5. You can also view the InfoBar to see a summary of the responses, such as Accepted, Declined, or Tentative.

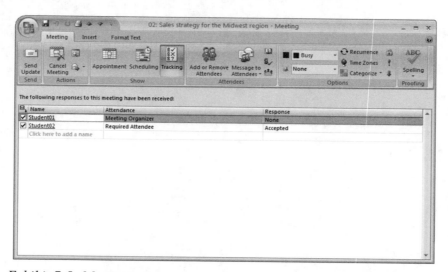

Exhibit 7-5: Meeting responses

Do it!   ## C-1: Reviewing meeting responses

Here's how	Here's why
1 Activate the Calendar	
2 Select the date from the Date Navigator	To see all the appointments for the day. If you belong to Group A, select next Monday. If you belong to Group B, select next Tuesday. If you are not in a group, select next Wednesday.
3 Open the meeting <xx>: Sales strategy for the Midwest region	1 attendee accepted, 0 tentatively accepted, 0 declined. (Double-click the meeting.) Be sure to select the meeting for which you're the organizer. The InfoBar displays the number of attendees who have accepted, tentatively accepted, and declined your meeting request.
4 Click **Tracking**	(On the Ribbon.) A list of all the invitees and their responses appears.
5 Save and close the meeting	To save the meeting and close the Meeting window.

Update a meeting

Explanation

You can send meeting updates if the date, time, or location changes for a meeting. Open the Meeting window, make your changes, and click Send Update. A meeting update message will be sent to each of the meeting attendees. The message will display the new information. The Reading Pane informs the attendee that no response is required and provides a Calendar button that can be used to view the updated meeting information in the Calendar, as shown in Exhibit 7-6.

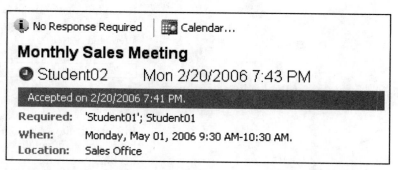

Exhibit 7-6: Updated meeting message in the Reading Pane

Do it!

C-2: Updating a meeting

Here's how	Here's why
1 Open a new Meeting window	Choose Actions, New Meeting Request.
2 Address the meeting request to your partner	In the To box, enter the name of your partner.
Specify the subject as **\<xx\>: Monthly sales meeting**	
Specify the location as **Sales office**	
3 Specify the start date as the first day of next month	
Specify a start time	If you belong to Group A, specify 9:00 A.M. If you belong to Group B, specify 11:00 A.M. If you are not in a group, specify 1:00 P.M.
Specify the end time as one hour later	
4 Send the meeting request	
5 Activate Mail	
Check for new messages	
6 Select the message with the subject \<yy\>: Monthly sales meeting	(If necessary.) The contents of the meeting request appear in the Reading Pane.
Click **Accept**	(The Accept button is in the Reading Pane.) To accept the meeting request from your partner.
	The Microsoft Office Outlook dialog box appears.
7 Observe the Microsoft Office Outlook dialog box	By default, Send the response now is selected.
Click **OK**	To send the response and close the Microsoft Office Outlook dialog box.
8 Activate Mail	If necessary.
Check for new messages	

9 Observe the message with the subject Accepted: <xx>: Monthly sales meeting

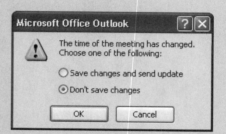

The message indicates that your partner has accepted the meeting request.

10 Activate the Calendar

Open the appointment with the subject <xx>: Monthly sales meeting

11 Change the start time to 30 minutes later

Save the meeting

The Microsoft Office Outlook dialog box appears.

Observe the Microsoft Office Outlook dialog box

The dialog box informs you that because the time of the meeting changed, you can either save the changes and send a meeting update, or you can discard the changes.

Select **Save changes and send update**

If necessary.

12 Click **OK**

To save the changes and send the update.

Close the Meeting window

13 Activate Mail

Check for new messages

14 Select the message with the subject Accepted: <xx>: Monthly sales meeting

Observe the Reading Pane

Notice that the time for the meeting has changed and the Reading Pane displays an informational message that no response is required. The Reading Pane also provides a Calendar button to view the updated meeting in your calendar.

Add or remove meeting attendees

Explanation

You can add and remove meeting attendees as needed from a meeting. To do so, open the meeting and click Add or Remove Attendees. Make your changes and click OK. Click Send Update and choose to send the update to the attendees who were added or removed, or to send the update to all attendees. Click OK to finish sending the update.

Do it!

C-3:   Adding meeting attendees

Here's how	Here's why
1 Activate Calendar	You'll add a meeting attendee and send an update to just the new attendee.
2 Double-click **<xx>: Monthly sales meeting**	
3 Click **Add or Remove Attendees**	
Select another student	
Click **Required**	
Click **OK**	
4 Click **Send Update**	
5 Verify Send updates only to added or deleted attendees is selected	Notice you can also select to send the update to all attendees.
Click **OK**	Only the new attendee will receive the meeting update.

Cancel meetings

Explanation

When you cancel a meeting, Outlook removes the meeting from your schedule. To cancel a meeting, select it in the To-Do bar and click the Delete button on the Standard toolbar.

The Meeting window appears. Notice that the Show As list is now set to Free and the Reminder list is set to None. To cancel the meeting and send a cancellation message to all the attendees, click Send on the Ribbon.

If a meeting is cancelled that you were planning to attend, you will receive a cancellation message. When the message arrives, click Remove from Calendar in the Reading pane to remove the meeting from your Calendar. You can also open the message and click Remove from Calendar on the Ribbon.

You cannot cancel a meeting without sending a cancellation message. This prevents attendees from showing up for a cancelled meeting.

Do it!

C-4:   Canceling a meeting

Here's how	Here's why
1 Select the appointment with the subject <xx>: Quarterly sales review	(In the To-Do bar.) This is the proposed meeting that was declined by your partner.
2 Delete the meeting	(Click the Delete button.) The Meeting window appears. You'll cancel this meeting and send a cancellation message to all attendees.
3 Click **Send Cancellation**	To send the cancellation message.
4 Activate Mail	If necessary.
Check for new messages	
5 Open the message with the subject Canceled: <yy>: Quarterly sales review	Notice the meeting date. You'll remove this appointment from your calendar.
Click **Remove from Calendar**	(On the Ribbon.) To delete the meeting from your Calendar.
6 Activate the Calendar	
From the Date Navigator, select the date when the meeting was scheduled	The cancelled meeting has been removed. If you belong to Group A, select tomorrow's date. If you belong to Group B, select the day after tomorrow. If you are not in a group, select the date three days after the current date.

Unit summary: Meeting requests and responses

Topic A   In this topic, you used the Calendar to **plan a meeting**. Then you learned about the features of the Meeting window. You created and sent a **meeting request**, which contains all the details of a meeting proposal, such as time, date, and subject.

Topic B   In this topic, you learned about the **components** of a **meeting request**, such as the attendees, date, time, location, duration, and subject of the meeting. You learned how to **accept** or **decline** a meeting request. You also **proposed a new time** for the meeting.

Topic C   In this topic, you learned how to **review** meeting responses by using the **Tracking button** in the Meeting window. You also learned how to update a meeting and how to add and remove meeting attendees. Next, you learned how to **cancel a meeting**.

Independent practice activity

In this activity, you'll create and send a meeting request. You'll also open a meeting request and propose a new time. Finally, you'll accept a proposed time change.

1 Create a meeting request with the subject **<xx>: World wide sales strategy** for next Tuesday. Send the meeting request to your partner.

2 Open the meeting request that you receive from your partner.

3 Propose a new time, and send the meeting request.

4 Accept the proposal. (*Hint:* Open the new-time-proposed message, and click **Accept Proposal**.)

5 Close Outlook.

Review questions

1 What is the advantage of using the Plan a Meeting window before mailing a meeting request?

2 How do you send a meeting request without using the Plan A Meeting window?

3 What are the four types of meeting attendees?

4 How do you accept a meeting request?

5 What is the main difference between accepting a meeting request and declining one?

6 Do you always have the option of proposing a new date and time if you are invited to a meeting that doesn't work with your schedule?

7 How do you add or remove a meeting attendee?

8 As the meeting organizer, how can you easily see all of the invitees' responses to your meeting request?

9 As the meeting organizer, which of the following options are not available when you cancel a meeting? (Choose all that apply.)

A A cancellation message is sent to only attendees who accepted the meeting.

B A cancellation message is sent to all attendees.

C A cancellation message is sent to no one.

D The message is deleted from your Calendar.

Course summary

This summary contains information to help you bring the course to a successful conclusion. Using this information, you will be able to:

A Use the summary text to reinforce what you've learned in class.

B Determine the next courses in this series (if any), as well as any other resources that might help you continue to learn about Outlook 2007.

Topic A: Course summary

Use the following summary text to reinforce what you've learned in class.

Unit summaries

Unit 1

In this unit, you learned how to start Outlook. You learned how to use the **buttons** and **icons** in the **Navigation pane** to access the various panes and folders. You also learned how to use the **Reading pane** and the **To-Do bar**. Next, you learned how to use the **Advanced toolbar**. Then you learned how to **use** and **customize Outlook Today**. Finally, you learned how to use the different help options, such as the **Type a question for help box** and the **Microsoft Office Outlook Help window**.

Unit 2

In this unit, you learned how to configure various **e-mail accounts**, such as **Exchange Server, HTTP, POP3**, and **IMAP**. Next, you learned how to create, send, reply to, and check the spelling and grammar in messages. You also learned how to attach a file to a message. You learned how to forward, delete, and restore messages. Finally, you learned how to preview, read, and save an attachment.

Unit 3

In this unit, you learned how to set **sensitivity** and **importance levels** for a message. Next, you learned how to **flag** messages. Then, you learned how to set the options to receive a **read receipt**. You also learned how to create and use **Search Folders**. Finally, you learned how to customize **page setup** and how to print messages.

Unit 4

In this unit, you learned how to use the **Contacts pane** and **folder** to **create** and **edit** contacts. Then you learned how to use the various **views** to organize their contacts. You also learned how to create and use **distribution lists**. Finally, you learned how to create, modify, and send **electronic business cards**.

Unit 5

In this unit, you learned how to add and edit **tasks** by using the Tasks folder and the To-Do bar. You also learned how to add a **recurring task**. Next, you learned how to mark **completed tasks** and insert a task into a message. You also learned how to view the tasks by using various **views**. In addition, you learned how to assign tasks. You also learned how to accept or decline a task request. Finally, you learned how to send a **task status report** for an assigned task and how to track an assigned task.

Unit 6

In this unit, you learned how to use the **Calendar** to set up an **appointment**. You also learned how to add and modify a **recurring appointment**. Then you learned how to insert an appointment into a message. Next, you learned how to delete and restore appointments. You also learned how to use the various **Calendar views**. You learned how to change the **workday times** and how to add a **time zone**. Finally, you learned how to add **multi-day events, annual events**, and **holidays** to a Calendar.

Unit 7

In this unit, you learned how to plan a meeting. You also learned how to create and send **meeting requests**. Next, you learned how a **meeting workspace** functions. You also learned how to read and accept a meeting request. Then you learned how to propose a new time for a meeting and how to decline a meeting request. You also learned how to review meeting responses. Next, you learned how to update and how to cancel a meeting.

Topic B: Continued learning after class

It is impossible to learn to use any software effectively in a single day. To get the most out of this class, you should begin working with Outlook 2007 to perform real tasks as soon as possible. Course Technology also offers resources for continued learning.

Next courses in this series

This is the first course in this series. The next course in this series is:

- *Outlook 2007: Advanced*

Other resources

For more information, visit www.course.com.

Outlook 2007: Basic

Quick reference

Button	Shortcut keys	Function
		Opens the Notes pane and folder.
		Opens the Shortcuts pane and folder.
		Lists all the folders in the Folder List pane.
		Opens the Outlook Today page.
		Represents an unread message.
		Represents a message that's been read.
		Represents a message that's been read and replied to.
		Represents a message that's been read and forwarded.
		Represents a message that contains a file attachment.
		Represents a flagged message.
B	CTRL + B	Makes the selected text bold.
Copy	CTRL + C	Copies the selected text.
Paste	CTRL + V	Pastes the selected text.
U	CTRL + U	Underlines the selected text.
✕	DELETE	Deletes any selected Outlook item.

Button	Function
	Opens the address book.
Day	Shows all the appointments for a day.
Week	Shows all the appointments for a five-day workweek.
Month	Shows all the appointments for the current month.
	Assigns a color category to a Calendar item, such as an e-mail message, task, or appointment.
	Opens the Plan a Meeting window.
Page ▾	Helps you send a page from Internet Explorer.
	Displays a list of commonly used file commands, such as New Message, Send, and Save.

Glossary

Address book

Contains the names of people with whom you frequently communicate.

Annual event

An event that occurs every year on a specific day. A birthday is an example of an annual event.

Appointment

A calendar item that contains meeting information such as date, start time, end time, and location.

Attachment

A file that is transmitted along with an e-mail so the recipient can see the file in its original format.

Contact

A person with whom you have either a business or a personal relationship. You manage information about each contact, such as the person's name, address, telephone number, e-mail address, Web page address, company name, birthday, and anniversary.

Contacts

Also referred to as the *Outlook Address Book*, is an address book that is private for each user. You can use Contacts to add e-mail addresses of the people with whom you frequently communicate.

Date Navigator

A miniature calendar that's used to select a date to be displayed in the Calendar. The To-Do bar also contains a Date Navigator.

Distribution list

A group of e-mail addresses under a single entry, enabling you to send one message to multiple recipients.

E-mail

An electronic message sent from one computer to another.

E-mail account

Contains the information that identifies a user so that the user can send and receive e-mail messages. A user can have more than one e-mail account. To access an e-mail account, a user should have a user name and a password.

E-mail postmarking

A feature that incorporates a digital postmark into messages that can be used to help reduce the amount of spam in your Inbox. Messages without postmarks are sent to the Junk E-mail folder.

Event

An activity that lasts for a period of one or more days and that can be added to the Calendar. There are two types of events in Outlook: multi-day and annual.

Folder pane

The middle pane of the Outlook window that displays the Folder Contents list.

Global Address list

An Exchange Server address book that contains all the users, groups, and distribution-list e-mail addresses in your organization. All the users in an organization have access to the Global Address list. Only the Exchange Server administrators can edit this address book.

Home page

The first Web page that appears when you visit a Web site or open a folder.

Hypertext Transfer Protocol (HTTP)

A set of rules used for communicating over the Internet.

Importance

The priority of a message. When you set the Importance level of a message to High, the red exclamation mark at the end of the message tells the recipient that the message needs an immediate response.

Inbox

One of the most frequently used Outlook folders that contains all messages that you receive. You can read, create, reply to, forward, and delete messages in this folder.

InfoBar

Located at the top of a message in the Reading pane or Message window, this area indicates the action taken on the message, along with the date and time.

Instant Messaging

An Office 2003 feature that enables you to send and receive messages instantly over the Internet or an intranet. This can be significantly faster than e-mail, in which messages are not received until they are downloaded from a server.

Instant messengers

Standalone programs that you can download and install to use when sending instant messages.

Internet Message Access Protocol (IMAP)

A set of rules used to retrieve e-mail messages from a mail server. Similar to POP3, IMAP contains some additional features such as searching messages by keyword before downloading them.

Internet Service Provider (ISP)

A company, such as America Online (AOL), MSN, and Earthlink, that supplies Internet connectivity services to individuals, businesses, and other organizations.

Intranet

A network, based on TCP/IP protocols, that belongs to an organization and that is accessible only to the organization's members or any other authorized users.

Item

Any e-mail message, contact, or task created in Outlook. Items are stored in folders, such as Inbox, Calendar, Contacts, Tasks, and Notes.

Junk e-mail

Unsolicited messages, such as business promotions, advertisements, and messages with adult content.

Live Meeting

A technology that enables you to participate in meetings over the Internet or an intranet.

Logging on

The process of gaining access to an e-mail account by entering the correct user name and password.

Meeting request

An invitation that contains all the details of a meeting proposal, such as time, date, and subject. These invitations are sent by e-mail to the invitees.

Meeting workspaces

Shared meeting Web sites that centralize all of the meeting information and materials needed in one place, so it's easily accessed by participants. Meeting workspaces require access to a Windows SharePoint Services team site.

Message flag

A flag symbol to the right of the message in the Folder Contents list that identifies the message for further action by inserting. When you flag a message, you can specify the action to be taken, the due date, and the time. Flagged messages appear in the Task list on the To-Do bar.

Microsoft Live Communication Server

An extensible platform that can deliver presence capabilities and instant messaging services through familiar user interfaces.

Microsoft Live Meeting

An online, real-time conferencing tool that you can use to take advantage of the Internet or your organization's intranet.

Windows Live Messenger

An application for sending and receiving instant messages.

Multi-day events

Events that last for more than one day.

Navigation pane

The leftmost pane in the Outlook window that's made up of three sections: the active pane, pane-switching buttons and icons, and a Configure buttons icon.

Organize page

A feature you can use to organize items by creating a rule, applying color, or displaying a view.

Outlook Address Book

Contains a private list of e-mail addresses and is automatically created from the contacts you create in the Contacts folder. When you update the contact information, the Outlook Address Book is updated automatically.

Password

A unique identifier that the user enters for security reasons.

Personal Folders file

The data file with a .pst extension that is used to store Outlook items and is located on your local hard drive.

Phishing message

A message that tries to convince you to enter personal information, such as your bank account or passwords. Phishing messages often have deceptive links that take you to spoofed (fake) Web sites.

Plan a Meeting feature

A calendar utility that helps you schedule meetings by finding available times for selected invitees and resources.

Post Office Protocol 3 (POP3)

A set of rules that are used to retrieve e-mail messages from a mail server. Similar to IMAP.

Protocol

A set of rules or standards designed to help computers communicate with each other through a network or on the Internet.

Range of recurrence

The start and end period of a recurring task or appointment.

Reading pane

A pane in the Outlook window that displays e-mail messages.

Recurrence pattern

The frequency with which a task or appointment occurs. For example, the task or appointment can occur annually, monthly, weekly, or daily.

Recurring appointment

An appointment or meeting that occurs regularly.

Recurring task

A task that needs to be performed on a regular basis.

Search Folders

Used to store messages in a specific category or based on a specific condition.

Sensitivity

A message classification that indicates messages that contain personal or highly sensitive content. There are four levels of sensitivity: Confidential, Private, Personal, and Normal (default).

SharePoint Services

A technology that enables aggregation, collaboration, and search capabilities for people, teams, and information.

Task

An Outlook item that keeps track of activities that must be completed within a specified period of time. A task has a current status, which can be In Progress, Not Started, Waiting on someone else, Deferred, or Completed.

Task list

A section of the To-Do bar that displays the tasks for the current date.

Task request

An e-mail message asking the recipient to complete a task.

Tasks folder

The folder that's used to create tasks and monitor their status.

To-Do bar

A pane in the Outlook window that displays the Date Navigator, upcoming appointments, and tasks.

User name

A unique identifier for every user.

View

The way data appears in a folder, such as Calendar, Contacts, Tasks, Notes, and Journal.

Index

V